T0319099

Cambridge Elements

Elements in the Politics of Development
edited by
Rachel Beatty Riedl
Einaudi Center for International Studies and Cornell University
Ben Ross Schneider
Massachusetts Institute of Technology

Mario Einaudi
CENTER FOR
INTERNATIONAL STUDIES

MIT CENTER FOR INTERNATIONAL STUDIES

A CHINESE BUREAUCRACY FOR INNOVATION-DRIVEN DEVELOPMENT?

Alexandre De Podestá Gomes
Constructor University, Bremen and State University of Campinas, Brazil

Tobias ten Brink
Constructor University, Bremen

CAMBRIDGE
UNIVERSITY PRESS

Shaftesbury Road, Cambridge CB2 8EA, United Kingdom

One Liberty Plaza, 20th Floor, New York, NY 10006, USA

477 Williamstown Road, Port Melbourne, VIC 3207, Australia

314–321, 3rd Floor, Plot 3, Splendor Forum, Jasola District Centre, New Delhi – 110025, India

103 Penang Road, #05–06/07, Visioncrest Commercial, Singapore 238467

Cambridge University Press is part of Cambridge University Press & Assessment, a department of the University of Cambridge.

We share the University's mission to contribute to society through the pursuit of education, learning and research at the highest international levels of excellence.

www.cambridge.org
Information on this title: www.cambridge.org/9781108972215

DOI: 10.1017/9781108975902

First published 2023

A catalogue record for this publication is available from the British Library.

ISBN 978-1-108-97221-5 Paperback
ISSN 2515-1584 (online)
ISSN 2515-1576 (print)

Additional resources for this publication at www.cambridge.org/Gomes-tenBrink.

A Chinese Bureaucracy for Innovation-Driven Development?

Elements in the Politics of Development

DOI: 10.1017/9781108975902
First published online: August 2023

Alexandre De Podestá Gomes
Constructor University, Bremen and State University of Campinas, Brazil

Tobias ten Brink
Constructor University, Bremen

Author for correspondence: Alexandre De Podestá Gomes, agomes@con structor.university; gomes21@unicamp.br

Abstract: This Element scrutinizes the attempts by the Chinese party-state bureaucracy since the 2000s to advance innovation and technological upgrading. It examines insights from the developmental state debate – the need for a bureaucracy to achieve internal coherence and the capacity of that bureaucracy both to forge coalitions between bureaucrats, businessmen, and scientists and to discipline domestic companies. Moreover, it assesses efforts to foster technological upgrading in the semiconductor and electric vehicle industries. While there are significant differences between China and earlier successful developmental states, with the former facing problems such as the legacies of short-termism, limited monitoring capabilities, and flawed discipline over business, the authors find that, compared with other emerging capitalist economies, the Chinese bureaucracy has developed strong capabilities to advance "innovation-driven development." This Element seeks to provide avenues for comparing China with other late developers.

Keywords: China, innovation, bureaucracy, economic development, state–business relations

ISBNs: 9781108972215 (PB), 9781108975902 (OC)
ISSNs: 2515-1584 (online), 2515-1576 (print)

Contents

1 Introduction   1

2 The Chinese Bureaucracy and Innovation-Driven
  Development   11

3 Assessing Technological Upgrading: Semiconductors
  and Electric Vehicles   42

4 Conclusion   62

  References   67

Further supplementary material can be accessed at
www.cambridge.org/Gomes-tenBrink

1 Introduction

China's remarkable economic development experience distinguishes it from other emerging economies like Brazil or Mexico, and has seen it embark on a path that appears to resemble that of successful late developers such as Japan or South Korea. More recently, the People's Republic of China (PRC) has strongly emphasized the idea of "innovation-driven development," a strategy that has attracted much attention in the West. From the 2000s, and especially in the 2010s, this strategy was substantially strengthened. Several very large programs were launched, pushing for innovation-driven development, huge investments in science and technology (S & T), and targeted industrial policies in existing and emerging sectors, such as semiconductors and electric vehicles. The following statement from the Outline of the National Innovation-Driven Development Strategy (State Council, 2016a) summarizes the overarching rationale: "It is the nation's destiny to be innovation-driven. The core support of national strength is technological innovation capability. National prosperity follows from strength in innovation, and national misfortune follows from weakness in innovation."

This Element scrutinizes the attempts by the Chinese bureaucracy to foster technological upgrading and improve the innovation capacities of domestic businesses.[1] More specifically, we consider how the party-state bureaucracy has been reorganized since the 2000s and ask whether this has created sufficient leverage to achieve these ambitious aims. To evaluate the capabilities of the bureaucracy, we examine two crucial theoretical insights from the developmental state debate – the need for a bureaucracy to achieve internal coherence and the capacity of that bureaucracy both to forge coalitions between bureaucrats, businessmen, and scientists, and to discipline domestic companies. Moreover, we use evidence from China studies on how bureaucrats have impacted the country's development, and we draw on innovation studies focused on China. We complement this with findings from offline and

---

[1] We define innovation as "the implementation of a new or significantly improved product (good or service), or process, a new marketing method, or a new organizational method in business practices" (OECD, 2005: 46). Innovation policies overlap with the notion of industrial policy, which can be divided into three types: economy-wide (e.g., macroeconomic policies), multisectoral (e.g., infrastructure and R & D policies), and sectoral industrial policies (the promotion of specific sectors) (Wade, 2005). Although the third type is typically the main focus of industrial policy debates, the three types are intertwined and mutually supportive. The term "industrial policy" can therefore also include innovation policies, and vice versa. Indeed, "much of what is called innovation policy today may previously have gone under labels such as industrial policy, science policy, research policy, or technology policy" (Edler & Fagerberg, 2017: 5). In this Element, we use the terms innovation and innovation policy in a broader sense, that is, including industrial policy. In the sections focused on targeted sector-specific industry promotion, we use "industrial policy."

online fieldwork (before and during the COVID-19 pandemic), national and local statistical data, and expert interviews (see the online supplementary materials for more information).[2]

In a nutshell, our analysis suggests that the bureaucracy has strong capabilities to promote innovation when compared with other emerging capitalist economies. Indeed, today the PRC is outperforming all other middle-income countries with regard to innovation capacities. We scrutinize this performance by analyzing, first, attempts from the 2000s onward to strengthen internal bureaucratic coherence at the horizontal and vertical levels. Second, we assess the bureaucracy's efforts to ease information exchange with businesses as well as to promote the science–industry collaboration pivotal to technology transfer, and to discipline firms so that they move beyond a narrow, short-term focus on output growth. We then demonstrate strengths and weaknesses of technological upgrading in two critical industries, semiconductors and electric vehicles.

At first glance, with its attempts to achieve internal coherence and partner with businesses, the Chinese bureaucracy resembles developmental states in Japan or South Korea. But there is significant deviation from this model, too. As we shall see later, the bureaucracy is not capable of fully meeting the standards of internal coherence, coordinating pilot agencies, and developing productive state–business ties – critical components of technological upgrading that are identified in the developmental state debate. Nonetheless, in the fields under scrutiny, trends toward a relatively effective model of governance can be identified, including forms of bureaucratic learning and adaptative regulatory capacities (for earlier works leaning toward this interpretation, see Tsai, 2006; Heilmann, 2017; Zhi & Pearson, 2017). Over time, in an iterative way, the bureaucracy has been adjusting its engagement with nonstate actors, employing rational–instrumental measures to channel investments to potentially innovative areas and pegging the allocation of fiscal benefits to the upgrading performance of firms. These measures have been layered onto prior, less effective ways of governing economic and technology affairs. In other words, China's "hybrid adaptive" bureaucracy (Zhi & Pearson, 2017) has evolved over time – and

---

[2] Our methodology follows the approach of in-depth qualitative national case studies. To this end, we triangulate different primary and secondary data sources to trace and critically assess China's development experience as effectively as possible. Triangulating data sources also helps to increase the validity of results in the context of biased statistics, nontransparent party-state institutions, and difficulties acquiring representative data through qualitative fieldwork. With our analytical discussion, we seek to foster academic understanding, and, linked to historical and configurational approaches to explanation, we are cautious about making strong causal claims. A list of semi-structured expert interviews conducted for this research, each lasting between one and three hours, can be found in the online supplementary materials.

probably more than many Western observers would be willing to accept.[3] Characteristic strengths resulting from relative elite unity, such as a long-term orientation at national level, autonomy, flexibility to change course (if required), evolving forms of merit-based governance, and learning capacities, along with weaknesses, such as multiple and at times contradictory goals for local bureaucrats, persistent short-termism, and flawed discipline over business, have amalgamated into an alternative "real type" of bureaucracy that is nevertheless supportive of technological innovation.

Our findings suggest that the Chinese bureaucracy does not emulate Western "good governance" policy prescriptions nor does it resemble a Weberian ideal type of bureaucracy. This is puzzling, because China's rise coincided precisely with the promotion of the "good governance" agenda – the call for strong enforcement of well-defined private property rights, transparent and accountable policymaking, and the rule of law more broadly in order to make markets work efficiently (World Bank, 1994; Mungiu-Pippidi, 2020). The Chinese experience has been more strongly characterized by blurred boundaries between the state and business, and deviations from the rule of law ideal. As Ang (2017a) argues, bureaucrats often act in an entrepreneurial fashion, seeking additional sources of income from outside the formal budgetary apparatus, a behavior commonly endorsed by the state (see also Painter, 2012).

Our research focuses on the period from the 2000s to 2022. It is here that we observe the emergence and consolidation of the "innovation-driven development" strategy. This is not to say that there are no inconsistencies and variations within this period, but rather that these can be understood as part of, and connected to, the same broadly defined innovation strategy. Hence, we depart from interpretations that perceive the rise of Xi Jinping in 2013 as a self-evident and unquestionable periodization criterion when studying China's recent political economy. As Hsueh (2022: 13) argues, "the reinforcement of the central state's role in strategic sectors, which contribute to the national technology base ... predates the rise of Xi."

Moreover, we do not perceive the reforms from the 2000s onward, including the post-2013 period, as an outright suppression of business, in general, or of the market's allocative function. Guided by the innovation paradigm, the state has heavily invested in the creation of whole new industries, especially at the technological frontier, and thus engendered new spaces for capital accumulation and new profit opportunities for private companies. Furthermore, we observe state policies incentivizing business to invest in R & D and in sectors more

---

[3] As "perhaps no issue more effectively unites policy-makers, executives, and the urban public in China than the need to propel China into a high-technology future" (Naughton, 2018: 363), bureaucratic coherence is stronger than in other policy fields, such as healthcare.

likely to generate technological upgrading, such as high-tech manufacturing, while disincentivizing or even penalizing business in sectors with poorer prospects for technological upgrading. The party-state is not promoting an indiscriminate assault on business, but rather selectively promotes some activities – those linked to innovation goals – to the detriment of others. The period under scrutiny thus does not represent the "end of the reform era" (Minzner, 2018), but rather a new stage of ever-changing state–market relations in which more state does not necessarily mean less market. In fact, the "reform and opening up" (*gaige kaifang*) strategy was never meant to generate a laissez-faire economy in the first place,[4] and has always been closely associated with a conscious effort to (re)build the party-state in order to steer economic development (Shue, 1994).

In Section 1.1, we introduce assumptions from the literature, which structure the empirical parts of this Element – and, in line with our interest in de-exoticizing China, thereby place it in a broader comparative perspective. In Section 2, after briefly summarizing the legacies of the 1980s and 1990s, in which the bureaucracy was nowhere near the ideal of a developmental state, we focus on bureaucratic reorganization from the 2000s onward, our main period of analysis. This reorganization was driven by the assessment that the country should have more clearly defined long-term strategies for innovation, and could no longer rely on what was perceived as the dispersed and uncoordinated behavior of local governments, an underdeveloped S & T system, and the short-term orientation of many businesses and local bureaucrats. In the early 2000s, most domestic firms lacked innovative capabilities and exports were often low value-added, while foreign firms dominated high value-added segments. As we will demonstrate, while the PRC still wrestles with features of this earlier reform era, which we dub "growth by any means" – particularly the short-termism of business and local governments, and some of the worst effects of state capture – recent bureaucratic efforts should be seen as attempts to change the economy's pattern of accumulation to one in which the bureaucracy seeks to steer investments toward domestic industries that are more prone to innovation, instead of supporting poorly coordinated investments into whatever generates GDP growth in the short run.[5]

---

[4] The notion that "reform and opening up" should be seen as a progressive effort toward a free-market economy can be found in popular discourses and in academic literature. Gang & Woo (2009), for example, argue that the aim of economic reform in China and other transitional economies is to move from a centrally planned to a modern market economy. This is achieved when *all* the dimensions of the economy are *completely* reformed, that is, when "total coherence" is achieved (Gang & Woo, 2009: 361).

[5] Coming from a critical normative perspective, it should be emphasized that even the most "successful" development process is ugly when examined close up. This holds for any such process and its dirty realities and paradoxes, of course, not just China's.

Section 3 assesses the efforts to promote technological upgrading in two critical industries – semiconductors, an existing industry in which domestic businesses are trying to catch up with leading global players, and electric vehicles, a new industry, fraught with uncertainty, where Chinese firms are already attempting to become global technology leaders. We thereby engage with recent studies highlighting the challenges developmental bureaucracies face when promoting technologies at the global frontier (Wong, 2011; Kim, 2020). Despite higher technological uncertainty in the electric vehicles case, we find that China has advanced farther here than in semiconductors, due to an interplay of bureaucratic factors with industry characteristics. We argue that China's system of decentralized governance and experimentation – features that deviate from the canonical developmental state model – is more conducive to technological upgrading in emerging industries characterized by the absence of well-established global leaders, such as electric vehicles. In the case of semi-conductors – a mature industry which is already highly consolidated worldwide with a few very large and well-established players – a more centralized system, capable of preventing a dispersion of state funds and promoting catch-up, would probably be more suitable. Moreover, practices from the "growth by any means" phase persist in both industries, creating weaknesses in disciplining business and incentives for local governments to attract investments without necessarily focusing on technological upgrading. Section 4 concludes the Element and outlines future research avenues.

1.1 Insights from the Developmental State Debate

Despite considerable regional heterogeneities, it is an inescapable fact that the PRC has achieved enormous economic development. This trajectory has been characterized by the constant involvement of the state in the economy and strong ties between bureaucrats and business (Oi, 1995; Blecher & Shue, 2001; Duckett, 2001; Kroeber, 2016; ten Brink, 2019; Chen & Rithmire, 2020), in a marked deviation from the assumptions of mainstream economics.

These deviations lead us to engage with the more heterodox developmental state tradition with its insights into the role played by a fundamental actor in *any* development process: the state bureaucracy. Originating from analyses on late industrialization in the second half of the twentieth century, namely in Japan, South Korea, and Taiwan, and later expanding the focus to examine other, unsuccessful development trajectories, this provides a fruitful avenue for assessing the role of China's bureaucracy (Johnson, 1982; Amsden, 1989; Wade, 1990; Evans, 1995; Haggard, 2018; for a critical perspective on this literature, see Kang, 2002). A core feature of developmental states, following the original work of Johnson (1982), is its bureaucracy. While developmental states can be characterized by other significant features, such as the overriding priority placed on economic growth, the implementation of targeted industrial policies, the mobilization of funding for strategic industries, and policies that defy, rather than follow, a country's comparative advantages, bureaucrats play a crucial role in steering economic development in general, and innovation in particular. Both the internal organization of a bureaucracy and its ties with business are key variables for understanding economic development and, ultimately, innovation capacities and the potential to graduate to higher income levels. At first glance, China's experience since the 1980s resembles these earlier successful and frequently authoritarian developmentalisms. However, as we shall see, there are important differences (on the related scholarly debate, see White, 1993; Tsai & Cook, 2005; Howell, 2006; Beeson, 2009; Walter & Zhang, 2012; Knight, 2014; Ang, 2017b).

A starting point for understanding the importance of bureaucracies is the pervasiveness of market failures and the acknowledgment that the market is just one of many institutions that constitute capitalism (Chang, 2002; see also Polanyi, 2001). In the context, in particular, of the promotion of technological upgrading and innovation, the state may be required to take an active role and drive the direction of technological change by shaping and creating new markets (Mazzucato, 2016). Admittedly, neoclassical economists have developed an influential argument – linked to the "good governance" agenda introduced earlier – which challenges the idea of "governing the market" (Wade, 1990). It emphasizes the risk of "government failures" whenever the state interferes in the relative prices of the economy. As the state meddles in economic activity, the argument goes, problems related to state capture and rent-seeking come to the fore. Well-connected players become rent recipients and start to receive preferential treatment due to their political connections, regardless of their efficiency. Moreover, governments simply do not have the right information to decide which industry is the most promising, and thus deserving of support (Pack & Saggi, 2006). The result is ultimately misallocation of resources and corruption (Krueger, 1990).[6] The neoclassical argument must be taken seriously, of course. Indeed, key thinkers in the developmental state debate have provided fine-grained answers (see Haggard, 2018). To start with, information problems, for instance, can be reduced through mechanisms of information exchange with business. Since, however, close connections with business invite rent-seeking and state

---

[6] The way forward should be the establishment and enforcement of private property rights, rule-based institutions that regulate relations between the state and business, and a competitive electoral democracy (see Acemoglu & Robinson, 2012; for critical views, see Moore & Schmitz, 2008; Khan, 2012; Painter, 2012).

capture, these need to be mitigated as effectively as possible by a coherent bureaucracy capable of disciplining business, an ability which can only develop effectively in exceptional circumstances.

1.1.1 Horizontal and Vertical Bureaucratic Coherence

While a developmental bureaucracy can in principle promote the long-term goals of economic development and innovation, it cannot be assumed to always function in line with those overriding goals. Rather, the successes of East Asian economies were predicated on bureaucratic coherence, characterized by the existence of leading ministerial agencies (Johnson, 1982; Wade, 1990). "Pilot agencies," such as the Ministry of International Trade and Industry (MITI) in Japan or the Economic Planning Board (EPB) in South Korea, gained particular importance and were positioned above specialized bureaucracies. Bureaucratic conflict between ministries is considered harmful, and hence there is a need to overcome the difficulties of *horizontal* coordination across ministries to achieve interministerial coherence (Evans, 1995). In order to maintain bureaucratic coherence over longer periods, these pilot and other state agencies must be staffed with bureaucrats recruited based more on technical competence than on patron–client relations or political ideology, allowing policies to be formulated by a professional technocracy (Migdal, 1988; Haggard, 2018; for further discussion on state capacity and performance, see Centeno et al., 2017).

Moreover, bureaucratic coherence is not limited to the central bureaucracy, but also applies to the *vertical* dimension of the state (see Evans, 1995: 54, 72). This is particularly important for large, heterogenous latecomer economies, such as China (or Brazil and India; see Montero, 2001; Sinha, 2003), where effective policy implementation depends on the behavior of lower-level bureaucracies. The more vertically fragmented bureaucracies are, the higher the chances of implementation failure.

In the case of China, the study of central–local relations has attracted much scholarly attention, highlighting both positive effects of the leeway that subnational governments enjoy when it comes to economic governance and negative effects such as noncompliance with central directives, which hamper policy implementation (Lieberthal & Lampton, 1992; Shirk, 1993; Chung, 2000, 2015; Yang, 2004; Heilmann, 2008; Mei & Pearson, 2014). The center uses two main tools to guarantee vertical coherence: a system of fiscal decentralization and the so-called cadre evaluation system. The first provides the fiscal incentives for local officials to behave in accordance with goals set by the center, and the second allows the central government to monitor local bureaucrats and then reward or punish them depending on their achievements.

As we will see, problems emerge when there is a fiscal mismatch between revenues and expenditures at the local level, when the cadre evaluation system does not reach the lower levels effectively, or when the center sets contradictory targets for local bureaucrats. Unsurprisingly, scholars who perceive China as yet another developmental state normally emphasize the effectiveness of these tools (Knight, 2014), while more skeptical scholars highlight the problems found in the vertical dimension of bureaucratic coherence (Howell, 2006; Beeson, 2009).

To evaluate bureaucratic coherence, we first analyze a horizontal dimension, namely, whether, and to what extent, something akin to a national pilot agency has been developed. Second, on the vertical dimension, we analyze whether the systems of fiscal decentralization and cadre evaluation make local bureaucrats work in tandem with central objectives.

1.1.2 Coalitions and Discipline

Developmental states have always been characterized by strong ties, or coalitions, with the business sector (Evans, 1995; Johnson, 1999; Woo-Cumings, 1999; Kohli, 2004; Haggard, 2018). For Johnson (1999: 60), "each side uses the other in a mutually beneficial relationship to achieve developmental goals and enterprise viability." In the context of ambitious innovative efforts, in particular, it is important to provide information that feeds back into the industrial and innovation policymaking process in order to tackle the aforementioned information problems. Moreover, scientists and research organizations must be integrated to promote science–industry collaboration and technology transfer (Cao & Suttmeier, 2017; Appelbaum et al., 2018; Fu et al., 2022).

Both bureaucrats and business people may develop a common interest in collaborating (Schneider & Maxfield, 1997; Moore & Schmitz, 2008; Leftwich, 2010). A valuable literature focusing specifically on functional networks between businesses and bureaucrats has emerged (Doner, 1992; Schneider & Maxfield, 1997; Schneider, 1998; Chibber, 1999; Doner & Schneider, 2000), arguing that state–business ties and consultative bodies are critical, especially to address the technical and informational needs that become very specific as the economy diversifies.

Undoubtedly, however, these relations can also be disruptive and rife with conflict between state and business groups, which do not necessarily comply with state directives (Migdal, 1988; Chibber, 2003). Therefore, an important prerequisite for successful patterns of state–business ties is what Amsden (1989) called "discipline." Her study on South Korea finds that in the context of industrial or innovation policies which distribute significant funds to business, the bureaucracy had to ensure that the latter would use those funds productively and in accordance with the overriding priorities set by the state. As she explains, "repeated support by the government" to business was "exchanged, de facto, for good performance" (Amsden, 1989: 16). Notably, the allocation of resources was tied to export performance – a target that was easy to measure and monitor, and difficult for business to manipulate (see also Stiglitz, 1996; Chang, 2006). More recently, scholars have utilized the concept of discipline to understand the successes of former middle-income countries such as Israel in promoting high-tech sectors and commercializing R & D (Maggor, 2021). Here, the bureaucracy demanded that recipients of state R & D funds produce locally (i.e., they should not outsource their production) and refrain from selling the resulting intellectual property to foreigners.[7]

The ability of the bureaucracy to reward good performers and punish under-performers was what distinguished South Korea from less successful late developers. Yet, this very ability not only depends on bureaucratic coherence, but crucially on the distribution of power between the state and business (Amsden, 1989: 147). In South Korea, successful disciplining from the 1960s onward was based on the relative weakness of both the traditional ruling classes and private entrepreneurs (Kohli, 2004; Khan, 2010). This diminished class conflict and allowed the state to fill a political vacuum, thereby creating elite unity (see Kay, 2002 for a comparison with Latin America). Just as professional recruitment and pilot agencies are fundamental to a coherent bureaucracy, state power over business is essential for discipline to work.[8]

The existence or nonexistence of this particular distribution of power between the state and business, which allows the former to discipline the latter, is not the result of any special set of smart policies enacted by policymakers, but rather a result of distinct historical circumstances (see Haggard, 2018: 47–53). Kohli (2004), for example, emphasized different types of colonial legacies: while Japanese colonialism bequeathed relatively coherent bureaucracies in South Korea and Taiwan, British colonialism left West Africa with weak bureaucracies and fragmented states, which mostly ended up being dominated by patrimonial relations. Another key variable is the existence, or not, of "systemic vulnerabilities" (Doner et al., 2005) related to geopolitical competition and conflict, and the resulting mechanism of "collaborating to survive"

---

[7] The example of Israel illustrates that export promotion is not the only feasible disciplining strategy for developing countries. In fact, Khan (2010: 74) remarks: "export promotion can also be done inefficiently, as Pakistan discovered in the 1960s" (at the time, the country was subsidizing low-quality exports). The key is to have a coherent bureaucracy capable of disciplining businesses in accordance with innovation goals.

[8] In contrast, during twentieth-century catch-up processes in Brazil and Turkey, bureaucrats were often afraid of monitoring and punishing businesses for fear of alienating supporters (Evans, 1995; Schneider, 1998).

(Schneider & Maxfield, 1997: 25; also see Migdal, 1988; Johnson, 1999). National security concerns and fears of external threats have often led national elites to take additional risks to consolidate control over society and to organize resources more effectively, prioritizing strong economic growth to catch up with established powers. In reform-era China, concerns over national security have always been entangled with the promotion of technological development, and they have intensified from the 2000s onward (see Hsueh, 2022). This stands in sharp contrast with the much less tumultuous geopolitical environment faced by most Latin American countries in the same period.

In this Element, we therefore analyze, first, whether, and to what extent, the bureaucracy has been able to forge coalitions with business and promote science–industry collaboration and, second, whether it is able to discipline businesses.

However, besides differences in size and internal socioeconomic heterogeneity, one important complication makes China a potentially deviant case: the role of foreign capital.[9] China's (re)emergence takes place in a different era, characterized by the increasing dominance of multinational corporations (MNCs) (Baek, 2005; Pirie, 2013; Doner & Schneider, 2016). Indeed, foreign firms have been particularly strong in high-tech manufacturing – in stark contrast to earlier East Asian economies. While this has provided Chinese companies with multiple "entry points" to acquire international technology, it has also created a fundamentally different reality to East Asia's earlier upgrading successes. As argued by Evans (1995) with regard to the Brazilian experience, disciplining transnational capital is trickier than disciplining domestic capital. Chen's (2018) study reveals how different local bureaucracies in China compete with each other and shows that local departments of international commerce, in particular, are more likely to forge coalitions with foreign capital. As a result, the promotion of indigenous technologies, as prioritized by the central state, faces resistance from the interests emanating from these local bureaucracies-cum-foreign capital coalitions, and discipline becomes harder to achieve. When analyzing discipline over business, we incorporate this reality.

This Element has certain limitations. Space constraints prevent us from discussing important topics in more detail. This applies, first, to the role of external factors and transnational influences, including how the fear of external threats motivated Chinese national elites to consolidate power over society. Foreign direct investment (FDI), and its ambiguous role for economic development, is also only touched on briefly (but see Gallagher & Shafaeddin, 2010 on

---

[9] Another important difference is the larger role for state-owned enterprises (SOEs), an aspect we cannot systematically tackle due to space constraints.

Mexico and China; and Liu, 2008 on the relationship between FDI and technology spillovers). Second, our somewhat elitist focus on the state and business does not account for the role of other societal actors, especially social movements and labor. In South Korea and Taiwan, for example, peasants and workers were effectively controlled as political forces during the catch-up processes. In reform-era China, independent trade unions have never flourished. Third, we had to forego a more in-depth discussion of other topics, including finance and the banking system, informality, agriculture, skill formation, and the education system, in favor of our more specific analysis of the bureaucracy and innovation.

We now move to Section 2, where, after summarizing legacies of the 1980s and 1990s, we consider that, despite success in economic growth, China suffered from the lack of an uncontested pilot agency, problems in policy implementation, limited monitoring capabilities, and enterprises detached from the domestic S & T system. As a result, in the early 2000s, a consensus gradually emerged within China's top leadership around a new innovation paradigm and a series of innovation plans, bureaucratic reforms, and new policies with ambitious goals were developed. We discuss these in Sections 3 and 4.

2 The Chinese Bureaucracy and Innovation-Driven Development

To better evaluate the bureaucracy's attempts to support innovation-driven development from the 2000s onward, we first introduce key legacies from the 1980s and 1990s reform era.

2.1 "Growth by Any Means": Reform Legacies, 1978–2000

From the end of the 1970s, China's move away from Maoist planning toward a more market-oriented economy was a gradual yet crisis-driven process of modernization. The economic strength of the neighboring developmental states in East Asia placed China under competitive pressure and instilled a fear of lagging behind its former vassal states. The region also served as a model for economic development. Domestically, facing the fallout of the Cultural Revolution and disappointing economic results as Maoism ended, important factions of the bureaucracy increasingly accepted any policies that would boost national output.

The "reform and opening up" strategy adopted from the late 1970s allowed greater leeway for the market as an allocative mechanism and for foreign capital in the economy. However, the actual scope and pace of this strategy has never been fully agreed upon, resulting in a "trial and error" policy process. Over time, the bureaucracy proved capable of adapting to new realities, which led to successful experimentation with markets and local entrepreneurialism. At the same time, the central bureaucracy was able to learn from these experiments and roll out local institutional and organizational innovations that fostered GDP growth nationally. Moreover, China's rise was aided by a changing geopolitical and world economic context, especially Sino–US rapprochement. Selective integration into the world economy had a massive impact on the country's transformation. In this context, China was in a favorable starting position, with certain established production infrastructures, and, given its very low income level at the time, a relatively skilled workforce with a basic general education.

In hindsight, this gradual transformation proved successful, especially when compared with the "shock therapy" path Russia had followed – the country's per capita GDP in 1989 would not be surpassed until 2007 (see Figure 2; also Weber, 2021). Figure 1 depicts China's GDP growth rate against low- and middle-income countries, and shows that its average growth rate was clearly higher than comparable countries from the early 1980s to 2020.

A comparison with specific middle-income countries confirms this trend. As Figure 2 shows, GDP per capita rose quickly from the 1990s onward, outpacing that of countries such as Indonesia in the late 1990s. Since the 2000s, China has been rapidly closing the gap with other middle-income countries and in the second half of the 2010s it overtook Brazil and Mexico, which in the early 1980s were way ahead of China. After relatively strong economic performance in the postwar period, many Latin American countries became stuck in a long phase of slow growth, in contrast to China's performance.

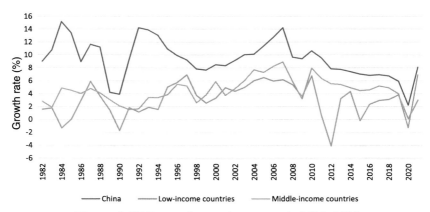

Figure 1 GDP growth rates (percentage), 1982–2021

Note: Annual percentage growth rate of GDP at market prices based on constant local currency. Aggregates are based on constant 2010 US dollars.

Source: World Bank data (https://data.worldbank.org/). The classification of low- and middle-income income countries follows World Bank criteria; see Hamadeh et al. (2022).

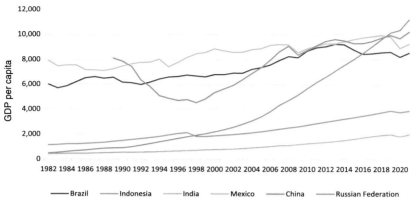

Figure 2 GDP per capita (constant 2015 US dollars), 1982–2021

Note: GDP per capita is gross domestic product divided by midyear population.

Source: World Bank data (https://data.worldbank.org/).

Of course, while this development is impressive, China continues to lag behind high-income countries. Previewing Section 2.2, with a GDP per capita of 11,188.30 US dollars in 2021, China's figure is roughly only 18 percent of that of the United States (61,280.39 US dollars) and 34 percent of that of South Korea (32,644.67 US dollars).[10]

To the surprise of Western observers, the reform process did not overhaul the PRC's political system writ large. Rather, the experimentalist pattern of "crossing the river by groping for stones" paved the way for a restructuring of the party-state in the interests of uncompromising development of productive forces and a vigorous process of capital accumulation (Saich, 2015; ten Brink, 2019). In short, from the 1980s onward, the bureaucracy was strongly geared toward "growth by any means" and implemented many administrative reforms, especially in the 1990s, to ensure state institutions supported market-oriented reform. Remarkably, when compared to the often violent political-power struggles in other emerging economies, the party-state elite remained a relatively coherent group throughout the reform period, despite rival factions and serious crises. Since large parts of the new ruling elite under Deng Xiaoping acknowledged the need to move away from Maoist policies, it was also possible to create a relatively homogeneous political ideology among decision-makers with a strong emphasis on economic development (Andreas, 2009; Weber, 2021).[11]

---

[10] Data are in constant 2015 US dollars and do not factor in differences in the cost of living in these countries. This therefore overestimates the gap between China and the United States.

[11] This relative homogeneity was based on the creation of a technocratic class comprising former Maoists, bureaucrats, and intellectuals, expressed as the need to be "red" and "expert" (Andreas, 2009). The party was never a monolith, though. Factions within the Chinese Communist Party

However, as we shall see, despite attempts to strengthen horizontal and vertical coherence, the country was far from a developmental state in this period. Unsurprisingly, given China's stage of economic development before the 2000s, the bureaucracy faced manifold complications. Local bureaucrats would often not comply with central directives, hampering policy implementation, and the short-termism of business and local bureaucrats undermined attempts to pursue longer-term goals.

2.1.1 Far from a Developmental State: The Central Bureaucracy

From the 1980s onward, a series of measures was implemented to build a developmental bureaucracy. We focus here on two areas: the buildup of functional government agencies at the horizontal level, and attempts to improve monitoring of bureaucrats to make them work in tandem with the objectives set by the center. This included the establishment of specific targets related to economic growth as the main criteria for evaluating cadres,[12] and the creation of a national civil service.

The central government system, inherited from the Maoist era, was restructured to adapt the bureaucracy to market conditions and to integrate more "specialist" policymaking (Burns, 1999; Yang, 2004).[13] While continuous reform is a ubiquitous characteristic of China's development, large-scale ministerial restructuring started rather late, in the 1990s. Most notably, the number of central ministries was reduced from forty to twenty-nine in 1998. In particular, the successor authorities of the industrial sectoral ministries were impacted. The Ministries of the Coal Industry, Machine Building, and the Chemical Industry, for instance, were incorporated into the State Economic and Trade Commission (SETC). In addition, the entire public sector underwent administrative reform that led to significant staff reductions (Yang, 2004).

In general, the restructuring could not resolve bureaucratic conflict between ministries and ministerial staff over jurisdictional authority. With regard to the fields under scrutiny, by the turn of the century the two main ministerial-level

---

(CCP) existed, and sometimes fierce battles erupted between them (Shambaugh, 2008). They were, however, all geared toward national development, as demonstrated in intellectual discourse: "The strands of discourse that were critical of the government represent different radicalized concepts of the official ideology. They are thus either much more nationalist or have a much stronger faith in the market" (Cho, 2005: 274, author's translation). On the intellectual battles between gradualist and shock therapy approaches to reform, see Weber (2021).

[12] We use cadre (*ganbu*) here to refer to any leading official in the government, administration, judiciary, party, SOEs, service units, and the military.

[13] See Bachman (1985) on the prereform origins of "specialist" policymaking epitomized by top cadres, such as Chen Yun, who were "prototypical of future generations of China's leaders who have advanced to positions of power on the basis of their mastery of particular areas of bureaucratic activity" (ix).

bodies responsible for organizing economic development were the State Development and Planning Commission (SDPC) and the SETC. Although the SDPC had a technocratic orientation, performing national coordination and regulatory roles, it fell short of the idealized pilot agency that policymakers were already envisioning based on Japan's MITI or South Korea's EPB. It faced pressures from both subnational polities and other central-level ministries and chronic understaffing – which in practice meant the SDPC had to rely on manpower and policy reports from other ministries and local governments (Lin, 2007). Sharp bureaucratic competition and the shifting of competencies resulted in fragmented policymaking (Heilmann & Shih, 2013).

While the ministerial reforms enabled the government to better regulate market expansion than those in other emerging economies (Nölke et al., 2020), the limits of the bureaucracy were clear when compared to successful developmental states, including in the S & T and education systems. Although some programs to address weaknesses in R & D had already started in the 1980s – such as the "863 program" in 1986 – the S & T system suffered from fragmentation and poor coordination. Many policies were disjointed, as exemplified by the promotion of R & D programs by different ministries following their own narrow agendas and overlapping funding for similar projects stemming from different agencies. Moreover, it took until 1998 to upgrade the State Science and Technology Commission into a more powerful organization – the Ministry of Science and Technology (MOST; see Zhi & Pearson, 2017). In this period the central state also withdrew its funding pledges from several government research institutes (GRIs), which were forced to find alternative sources of income in the market (Zhou & Liu, 2016; Liu et al., 2017).

With regard to attempts to improve monitoring of bureaucrats, a CCP National Work Conference in 1983 developed specific targets for the assessment of state and party cadres' performance, to replace the focus on political attitudes and work style that had been dominant during the Cultural Revolution. Material rewards and sanctions were also given weight, and performance indicators were introduced. It was not until 1988, however, that specific guidelines were issued for the annual evaluation of local cadres (Whiting, 2001). Of utmost importance for local cadres was the emphasis on industrial output targets and the introduction of financial bonuses for good performance. In many cases, these bonuses were higher than basic fixed salaries. Moreover, to encourage competition between different localities, cadres were assessed in relation to each other, and financial deductions could be imposed for poor assessments (Whiting, 2001; Edin, 2003).

Ultimately, this cadre evaluation system created an institutional link between the personal income of local bureaucrats and industrial performance, spurring the growth of local firms. Notably, the cadre evaluation system was managed by the CCP and its Organization Department. Edin (2003) notes that the promotion of successful local cadres became common practice in the 1990s (also see Huang, 1996).[14]

In addition, the Provisional Regulations on Civil Servants were adopted in 1993. These stipulated that public sector personnel were to be selected through open competitive examinations. This was expected not only to increase the quality of the civil service overall, but also to shield it from the influence of personal connections and particularistic interests (Burns, 1994; Heilmann, 2017).

In sum, the reforms geared the bureaucracy toward economic targets. Nevertheless, problems in the workings of the bureaucracy also surfaced. First, bureaucratic incoherence persisted in national agencies that focused on economic policymaking and S & T. Second, while there were some successful attempts to improve monitoring of bureaucrats, the system was still a long way from an effective bureaucracy. In particular, as we shall see, the system incentivized local cadres to focus on quantitative increases in production, without due regard to broader qualitative issues such as social welfare or technological upgrading.

2.1.2 Lack of Vertical Bureaucratic Coherence

Under Deng Xiaoping, local governments' leeway in implementing central policies or initiating their own was substantially increased (Chung, 2000). Effective local implementation became dependent on local officials' flexibility in taking local conditions into account when carrying out central policies. This has enabled policy experimentation by local bureaucrats, heralded as a key factor in explaining China's success throughout the reform period (Heilmann, 2008). While the PRC remained politically centralized, then, it favored strong administrative and fiscal decentralization.[15]

This system incentivized local governments to find alternative sources of income to fulfill their new expenditure responsibilities. In order to increase revenues, they promoted industries, in particular township and village enterprises, which served as a catalyst for the economy to "grow out of the plan" (Naughton, 1995). Evidently, this pleased central authorities, as it fostered growth and employment. However, the very same local autonomy also led to

---

[14] Party control of the state and the public sector of the economy typically manifests itself through the establishment of party cells, the nomination of organizational leaders by the Organization Department, and the control of those leaders through performance evaluations.

[15] In this Element, "local government" refers to the prefectural or city level. Space constraints prevent us from discussing the provincial, county, and township levels in detail.

collusion between officials and collective, hybrid, and private firms, resulting in fiscal underreporting and tax evasion (Whiting, 2001). As a result, total budgetary revenues as a proportion of GDP fell, and the central government's share of budgetary revenues vis-à-vis local governments decreased over time.

Thus, in 1994, the central government pushed for a structural reform of the fiscal system (Shen et al., 2012). The center's share of revenues rose as a result, as did the share of total budgetary revenue in GDP (see Figure 3). With greater fiscal capacity, the central government had more resources to promote investment in industrial and innovation policies, important features of the subsequent time period.

While the 1994 fiscal reform fostered recentralization of fiscal revenues, the trend of decentralization of expenditure responsibilities did not change significantly. This resulted in a fiscal mismatch: fiscal resources were highly centralized, administrative tasks and related expenditures were highly decentralized, and there were no formal institutions to guarantee that every local government had sufficient resources to fulfill the tasks it was allocated (Wong, 2009).

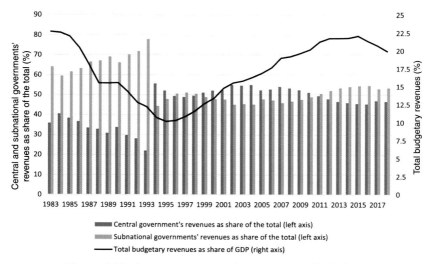

Figure 3 Budgetary revenues (percentage), 1983–2018

Note: the data excludes various forms of nonbudgetary revenues, such as land revenues and social insurance premiums. Naughton (2020) estimates that, after summing these items, China's total public revenues by the end of the 2010s could amount to 36 percent of GDP.

Source: Authors' calculation, based on the National Bureau of Statistics of China (NBS, 2020a).

The fiscal reform further incentivized local governments to drive growth. Deprived of resources and facing increased fiscal responsibilities, bureaucrats started to resort to a number of financing and development mechanisms, the essence of which was the conversion of rural to urban land (Tsui, 2011; Su & Tao, 2017). Moreover, they started to transfer the newly acquired land to so-called local government financial vehicles (LGFVs), which used it as collateral for bank loans. As a result, the focus shifted to urban infrastructure development, the establishment of industrial parks and development zones (Cartier, 2001; Wei, 2015).

Additionally, local states, especially in coastal regions, actively lured foreign capital as it was a quick way of boosting economic growth. Given the central government's primary focus on GDP growth, this once again pleased the authorities, despite associated drawbacks such as dependency on foreign technology.

In sum, then, local leeway was a double-edged sword: on the one hand, it enabled localities to come up with new strategies for GDP growth, and some deviation from central policies was actually desired by the center, as it allowed for experimentation (Zhou, 2020); on the other, local officials were driven by a short-term search for fiscal revenues, leading to systematic noncompliance and "selective implementation" (O'Brien & Li, 1999), especially when central objectives did not promise quick fiscal returns to local coffers. Moreover, the typically short tenures of leading local cadres encouraged a short time horizon (Zhang, 2019). These problems undermined the overall coherence of China's bureaucracy. If the center was to broaden its objectives and depart from its narrow focus on GDP growth, central–local relations would need to be revamped.

2.1.3 The Emergence of State–Business Coalitions and Their Limits

Chinese party-state elites had been in a dominant position for a long time. In the 1940s and 1950s, the state eradicated a powerful landlord class and a then nascent bourgeoisie (Shue, 1994). As the post-1978 process of capital accumulation took off, and with the gradual allowance and later encouragement of private ownership, an increasingly powerful group of entrepreneurs emerged.[16] But rather than challenging the supremacy of the party-state, mutually beneficial state–business ties emerged, especially at the local level. This laid the foundation for the promotion of information exchange with businesses, and later for attempts to push business toward meeting the goals of innovation.

Reform-era state–business interactions, often informal, supported a series of reforms that gradually gave legitimacy to the private sector. Local officials

---

[16] Chinese entrepreneurship comes in many different forms, from formally private to hybrid and modernized, listed SOEs that behave, in many ways, like private companies, but generally with better access to government support.

benefited from higher industrial output and thus fiscal revenues, and firms benefited from better access to land, bank loans, and production inputs. This interdependence underpinned rapid capital accumulation, with ultimate political control maintained by higher levels of the party-state (Whiting, 2001; Dickson, 2008; ten Brink, 2019).

A multiplicity of local-level coalitions emerged (Baum & Schevchenko, 1999; Howell, 2006). Oi (1995) and Blecher & Shue (2001), for instance, employ the expression "local developmental states," in which party leaders were at the helm of the local economy. They coordinated enterprises within their territory as if they were managing a diversified business corporation. Here, bureaucrats mostly intervened by creating an environment conducive to growth, but did not engage in business for profit. In contrast, as Duckett (2001) reveals, local bureaucrats also performed entrepreneurial roles: cadres started to invest directly and establish their own businesses, becoming "cadre entrepreneurs."

Local cadres' entrepreneurial role also extended to the S & T system. They connected with GRIs, which, at the time, were looking for partnerships with business in order to boost their revenues. As Zhou & Liu (2016: 38) argue, "desperate for funding and outlets for their research results, GRIs and universities set up their own spin-off enterprises, and encouraged scientists to leave their research positions and engage in commercial activities." Together with the construction of development zones and science parks to facilitate technology transfer, this formed the nucleus of numerous regional innovation systems.

Although local coalitions spurred investment in new enterprises and whole new sectors, they also promoted local protectionism, uncoordinated duplication of investments, support of often inefficient firms, and widespread corruption (Lu, 2000; Ong, 2012). Notably, while some successful spin-offs such as Legend/Lenovo marked a trend toward commercializing research and innovative firms, the bulk of firms lacked advanced technological capabilities. Primarily seeking short-term returns, most businesses were not willing to deal with the uncertainties of R & D investment, and thus were not motivated or able to commercialize R & D product technology from GRIs (Zhou & Liu, 2016: 38).

Moreover, linked to opening up the country to FDI, MNCs had, by the early 2000s, become very prominent, especially in high-tech sectors. This was in stark contrast with the experiences of East Asian developmental states, where the presence of foreign capital was negligible (Kroeber, 2016; Liu & Tsai, 2021). Local states were instrumental in offering MNCs advantages, such as tax breaks and easier access to land in development zones. China's attraction of FDI, while critical for the creation of jobs and output growth, produced disappointing results in terms of technological spillovers (Fu, 2015; Zhou & Liu, 2016; Liu & Tsai, 2021).

2.2 Toward Innovation-Driven Development: From the 2000s to the 2020s

By the early to mid-2000s, China's national ruling elite had largely acknowledged the necessity of promoting innovation more intensively and moving beyond a narrow focus on GDP growth. Gradually, a consensus began to form that companies were stuck in low value-added segments and dogged by weak technological dynamism. Concomitantly, domestic firms had poor R & D capabilities, undermining their ability to absorb foreign technology, while foreign-invested enterprises mostly conducted their core R & D at home (Fu, 2015; Zhou & Liu, 2016). This prompted the ruling elite to change strategy. Consequently, a series of grand innovation plans with ambitious goals were developed and attempts were made to reform the innovation-oriented segments of the bureaucracy (Heilmann & Shih, 2013; Naughton, 2020).

By the late 1990s, the government had already started to increase funding for GRIs and strengthen previously dispersed S & T programs. In parallel, an expansion of education, particularly tertiary, had been initiated (Postiglione, 2020). In hindsight, these activities were harbingers of a new strategy for technology development in which the central state would play a prominent role (Heilmann & Shih, 2013; Zhou & Liu, 2016; Naughton, 2020, 2021; Fischer et al., 2021). From the 2000s, and especially in the 2010s, this strategy was intensified, with "indigenous innovation" becoming a buzzword, and a paradigm change from external acquisition to internal knowledge creation taking place (Fu, 2015). The State Council launched several very large programs pushing for "innovation-driven development." Among them, the broad "National Medium- and Long-Term Program for Science and Technology Development (2006–2020)" (hereafter, MLP 2006), launched in 2006, the "Strategic Emerging Industries" program (2010), the "Made in China 2025" program (2015), the "Outline of the National Innovation-Driven Development Strategy" (2016), and the China Standards 2035 (2020), are worth highlighting. They were complemented by sector-specific industrial policies, such as those promoting the semiconductor and electric vehicle industries.[17]

These programs can be understood as part of a relatively coherent strategy based on long-term goals related to innovation and the promotion of high-tech industries,

---

[17] Among the manifold policies designed to foster innovation capacity, the following were key: the use of public procurement, where possible favoring domestic companies and technologies; subsidies; tax deductions for R & D expenditure; and the push for China's own technical standards in various industries. The funding was to come from the government's increased budgetary capacity, following the aforementioned tax reform (see Figure 3), investments by state-controlled enterprises, the leverage of the banking system (often by local governments), and a whole array of newly created "industrial guidance funds" and "state capital investment and operations companies," which in theory should operate like venture capital (Zhou & Liu, 2016; Naughton, 2020, 2021).

the creation of entirely new industries (e.g., electric vehicles), and the employment of new technologies to upgrade existing ones (e.g., semiconductors). The overarching rationale behind this strategy is the understanding that without strong technological capabilities, China will not become a developed, high-income economy.

At the same time, the ruling elite conceded that various problems could potentially thwart these ambitions. To begin with, the bureaucracy had no uncontested pilot agency capable of coordinating China's innovation policies effectively. The "growth by any means" phase bequeathed a series of fragmented policies in this field, exemplified by R & D programs being promoted by different ministries, each following their own narrow agenda (Cao & Suttmeier, 2017; Sun & Cao, 2021). The Chinese Academy of Sciences (CAS) is an illustrative example. The CAS comprised more than 100 institutes, many of them multifunctional, leading to redundancy and overlapping functions. Additionally, many had weak commercialization capabilities (Cao & Suttmeier, 2017; Liu et al., 2017).

Problems with coordination and coherence were not limited to the central level, however. Harmful effects of the process of decentralization became more obvious, especially in the implementation of industrial and innovation policies (Sun, 2007; Moore, 2014; van Aken & Lewis, 2015; Lee, 2017). The autonomy of local governments, coupled with the fiscal mismatch described earlier, and the emergence of ever more targets for the evaluation of local officials, led to failures in policy implementation in traditional industries such as steel (Sun, 2007) and automobiles (Huang, 2002). In the latter case, local bureaucracies would typically protect local companies, resulting in a significant fragmentation of the national market and the existence of relatively small companies unable to fully exploit economies of scale in the sector. Moreover, local governments often favored foreign enterprises, undermining the scope for indigenous innovation. Even with conscious efforts to attract more capital-intensive FDI and adopt a "trading market for technology" strategy, the results in terms of technological spillovers were disappointing. Domestic suppliers had made limited inroads in supplying higher value-added parts to Japanese or German automobile manufacturers, for example (Chin, 2018).

Compounding these problems, a series of corruption scandals involving top bureaucrats and party members were exposed (Lee, 2017; Miller, 2020; Wedeman, 2020), indicating the ineffectiveness of the bureaucracy's monitoring capabilities. While corruption in general was not new, cases of misconduct and fraud in China's S & T system were of particular concern (Cao & Suttmeier, 2017). The remuneration system for many S & T staff was characterized by relatively low basic salaries, incentivizing researchers to seek additional income from other projects, in which the boundaries between what was allowed and what was forbidden were vague (Liu et al., 2017). This echoes Ang's (2017a) general characterization of Chinese bureaucrats as incentivized to seek extra income sources from outside the formal budgetary apparatus.

Another problem was that businesses were typically disconnected from the S & T system, either preferring to use foreign technology or avoiding the inherent uncertainty of collaborating with research institutions on longer-term technological development (Liu et al., 2017; Suttmeier, 2020). Existing consultative bodies were often unsuitable for the new policy paradigm (Heilmann & Shih, 2013) and the state thus needed to strengthen the cooperation between (central and local) bureaucrats responsible for innovation and business.

Lastly, a more hostile international environment developed, even before the US–China "trade and tech war." China's (re)ascendance to power and potential global leadership, combined with the 2008 global financial crisis and subsequent shifts in US foreign policy (Hung, 2015; de Graaff et al., 2020), caused Sino–US relations to sour. This created pressure to forge strong domestic collaborations and encourage technological upgrading. Interrelated concerns about national security and the promotion of world-class indigenous technologies were exacerbated during this period, fostering the rise of what Hsueh (2022) calls "techno-security developmentalism" (see also Wang, 2022 on the growing importance of security concerns for the top leadership, and how these and economic development are seen as mutually reinforcing).

Against this background, a consensus on the new innovation paradigm emerged during the Hu-Wen administration, which was consolidated by the end of Hu Jintao's second term (2008–13). Notably, this consensus was formed prior to Xi Jinping coming to power in 2013, even though it is often associated with him and only took full shape under his rule (Heilmann & Shih, 2013; Lee, 2017; Miller, 2020).

2.2.1 Results of the Innovation Push

China's innovation strategy helped stimulate noticeable improvements in S & T indicators (see Figures 4 and 5). R&D capabilities have clearly improved. Total expenditure rose from nearly 160 billion yuan in 2001 to over 2 trillion yuan in 2020, with nearly 80 percent coming from enterprises.[18] From 2001, R & D intensity increased from less than 1 percent to 2.4 percent, albeit missing the 2006 target of achieving 2.5 percent by 2020. Likewise, total patent applications soared, from roughly 200,000 in 2001 to over five million in 2020. These quantitative improvements coincide with the rise of high-tech enterprises

---

[18] Disaggregating these numbers reveals a very uneven distribution of regional R & D expenditures – much higher than the national average in coastal provinces and lower in most western and northeast provinces – reflecting China's uneven development.

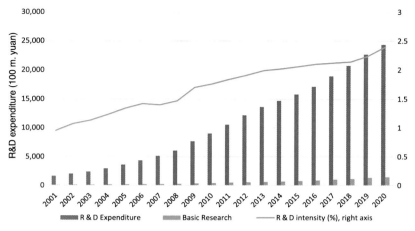

Figure 4 R & D expenditure (100 million yuan, 2020 prices)

Note: R&D intensity is measured as R&D expenditure as a percentage of GDP.
Source: NBS (various years)

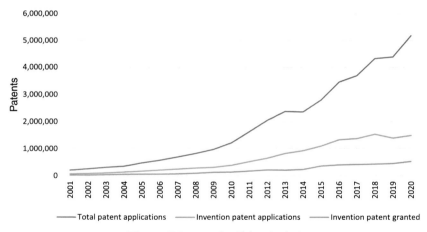

Figure 5 Patents in China (units)

Source: NBS (various years)

such as Huawei, BYD, and Xiaomi, huge infrastructure investments such as the high-speed rail network, and the buildup of regional innovation systems (Chen et al., 2021; Fu et al., 2022).

While these numbers are impressive, they hide shortcomings. Most companies are still dependent on foreign technology, as the recent conflict with the United States has revealed in the case of Huawei and its dependency on key semiconductor technology (Fuller, 2021). Often, as in other catch-up processes, Chinese technology emulates the functionality of existing foreign products. In fact, much of the success so far has been based on incremental improvements of existing products

(Breznitz & Murphree, 2011; Fu, 2015; Storz et al., 2021). This is reflected in the type of R & D that became prevalent in this period. "Basic research" and even "applied research" investment is still low compared to highly developed economies, with most investment going into improving existing products or processes, that is, "experimental development." Correspondingly, during this period the government actually reduced its contribution to gross R & D expenditure, from around 40 percent of the total to around 20 per cent. Hence, enterprises have borne the brunt when it comes to expenditure on R & D. That said, enterprises tend to be oriented toward quick commercialization and experimental development (Sun & Cao, 2021), as these options are less uncertain and promise financial returns in the short run.

When it comes to radical or breakthrough innovations – those with the potential to create new products and whole new markets – Chinese actors have made limited inroads (Appelbaum et al., 2018; but see Chen et al., 2021 who indicate that a trend change can currently be observed in some industries). Despite a remarkable increase in total R & D expenditure, then, a more fine-tuned focus on long-term investment is in order, with more state spending on basic research and better science–industry collaboration. Consequently, the recent 14th five-year plan (2021–5) calls for increased investment in basic research (Sun & Cao, 2021: 7). This also indicates that the bureaucracy is trying to learn from previous shortcomings.[19]

Moreover, many very large Chinese high-tech enterprises benefit from the protected domestic market. For example, Baidu and WeChat (Tencent) profit from their main competitors, Google and WhatsApp, being banned on the mainland, but have so far still failed to gain significant market shares overseas. The impressive rise in the total number of patent applications must also be interpreted with caution, as much was achieved thanks to utility models and designs. When the number of invention patents only is considered, the total number of patent applications is significantly lower (see Figure 5). In 2020, the number of invention patents made up less than one-third of total applications; and if we consider the number of invention patents actually granted, the share falls to roughly 10 percent. Empirical studies aiming to assess the real "innovativeness" of Chinese patents tend to agree that a large share of the surge in patents can be attributed to those of low quality (Hu et al., 2017; Schmid & Wang, 2017; Jiang et al., 2020; Interview #21). This should not, however, prompt us to downplay possible trend changes, given the astonishing pace at

---

[19] Of course, higher investment in basic research does not automatically produce more innovation, as exemplified in Brazil, where a proportionally large amount is invested in basic research, mainly conducted in universities but not well connected with industry (Interview #2, online supplementary materials; also see Paus, 2020: 675–76).

which the innovation system is developing.[20] As Jiang et al. (2020) argue, the Chinese innovation system is still maturing, and many of the current patenting efforts may only bear fruit later. In fact, considering China's current level of GDP per capita, the country's performance so far is remarkable.

Overall, then, China has made significant progress, and is now the world's most innovative middle-income country. According to the Global Innovation Index (2022), it is 11th in the ranking, outperforming other emerging economies such as Brazil, Russia, India, and South Africa, and on par with countries like Canada, Japan, and France.[21] However, there are significant differences between some areas where China is trying to push the global technological frontier – artificial intelligence, e-commerce, quantum computing, and electric vehicles, for instance (Chen et al., 2021; Mao et al., 2021) – and many other areas where it is still lagging behind global leaders (for a comparison with Brazil, Russia, India, and South Africa, see Dominguez Lacasa et al., 2019; Nölke et al., 2020). In Sections 2.2.2, 2.2.3, and 2.2.4, we show how these results are linked to attempts to reorganize the bureaucracy. We note, however, that the state measures to promote innovation covered here obviously do not preclude the importance of other complementary factors, such as the role of robust domestic demand, agglomeration economies, and industrial clusters in technological upgrading (see Gereffi, 2009; Zeng, 2011; Butollo & ten Brink, 2018).

2.2.2 Toward More Horizontal Coherence: Reforming Innovation-Oriented Segments of the Party-State

From the 2000s onward, a series of bureaucratic reforms were conducted to strengthen horizontal coherence. First, we focus on reforms targeting key ministries for innovation and industrial policy, and assess whether these reforms succeeded in creating something similar to a national pilot agency. Second, we focus on measures aimed at improving the professional recruitment and evaluation of bureaucrats, and third, we deal with reforms of the S & T system.

The period witnessed the rise of strong advocates of industrial and innovation policy to top decision-making positions.[22] This was influenced by an examination of international development experiences, including learning from

---

[20] Beyond China, patents have been criticized as an indicator of innovative performance, as firms can use other methods (e.g., secrecy) to ensure the commercial value of an invention, and not all patents are necessarily useful (Cohen et al., 2000).

[21] This ranking is based on a comprehensive range of innovation input and output indicators apart from patents.

[22] Another policy network, centered on ideas of imperative planning, largely disappeared in the 1990s (Heilmann & Shih, 2013: 18).

Japanese and Korean industrial policies – on top of and in interaction with local scholarship (see Huang, 2021). Learning was particularly strong in a policy network around the SDPC. While this policy network did not play a key role in the 1990s, when the overall institutional environment was less receptive to industrial policy and the state lacked fiscal resources, it proved to be decisive in "moving it to the center" from the 2000s onward (Heilmann & Shih, 2013: 12). One of its members, for instance, was Liu He, often seen as a leading specialist technocrat who supported industrial policies and had already achieved a notable status by the end of the Hu-Wen era, going on to consolidate his position as a top economic adviser during Xi's presidency. In 2010, Liu He publicly advocated the idea of "top-level design" (*dingceng sheji*). The core idea here is that the lack of policy coordination and the myriad bureaucratic interests inherited from China's earlier reform era were hampering the effectiveness of industrial and innovation policies. Another example is Wan Gang, a former academic who became Minister of Science and Technology (2007–18). Wan Gang was the most prominent promoter of the push toward electric vehicles (Zhi & Pearson, 2017; Interview #30).

The resolute support for the innovation paradigm from leading figures in top decision-making positions – including researchers-turned-officials with dense networks in the CCP, academia, and the world of business – was fundamental to guaranteeing policy consistency over time. Many countries in Latin America also attempted industrial and innovation policies in the same period but these suffered from a lack of continuity. As a result, a "stop-and-go" pattern of policy-making undermined their effectiveness (Paus, 2020). An illustrative case is the Brazilian policy on semiconductors. In 2008, under the Lula presidency (Workers' Party), a state-owned company, Centro Nacional de Tecnologia Eletrônica Avançada (CEITEC), was created. However, with the change of political power in the 2010s, industrial policy was rolled back and the expected government purchases of the company's products did not materialize. Although CEITEC eventually became the only Brazilian company capable of manufacturing semiconductors and managed to secure contracts with companies such as HP and Epson (Oliveira, 2020), by 2020 it was not making a profit and the incumbent government decided to close the company. After winning the general elections in 2022, the Workers' Party announced that it would attempt to repeal the measure that would result in the closure of CEITEC (Drummond, 2022). While the future of CEITEC is uncertain, the constant change in direction of Brazil's industrial policy certainly undermined the country's prospects for growth.[23]

---

[23] Another factor explaining Brazil's inconsistency is the absence (unlike China) of strong national security concerns.

At the institutional level, the PRC's top executive body, the State Council, was responsible for officially launching most large innovation programs, indicating some level of coherence in policy design. Beyond the State Council, a whole series of reforms have taken place since the 2000s in an attempt to reduce fragmentation. By the turn of the century, the two main ministerial-level bodies responsible for controlling and organizing industrial development and upgrading were the aforementioned SDPC and the SETC. Since they fell short of the model pilot agency found in developmental states (Lin, 2007; Heilmann & Shih, 2013), a new "super ministry" (*dabuzhi*) was formed in 2003, the National Development and Reform Commission (NDRC; see Yang, 2004; Wang, 2019). The NDRC was created through a merger of the SDPC with departments of the SETC. The aim was to control and organize industrial development, thereby improving coordination at the national level. This strong ministerial-level body of the State Council gave the impression that the PRC now had its own pilot agency.

However, while the NDRC became omnipresent and politically strong, exemplified by its macroeconomic role in combating the effects of the global economic crisis of 2007–8, it did not attain the status of an overarching and uncontested pilot agency able to coordinate policymaking by building consistent intrabureaucracy alliances. Bureaucratic conflict and interference in the jurisdiction of other ministries was still a reality and, "in effect, this meant that the NDRC lost some of its strategic influence with respect to economic and investment policy" (Heilmann, 2017: 78). Moreover, many of the NDRC's directors were former provincial governors or party secretaries, typically generalists who dealt with broad issues rather than technocrats with a specialized background in industrial or innovation policy (Wang, 2019). The NDRC thus became characterized more by the generalist scope of its operations, which primarily concerned macroeconomic management and administrative control over the economy. This made it increasingly unfit for the task of formulating industry-specific policies which demands specialist knowledge.

Several other powerful ministries became proactive players in the 2010s. The MOST, in particular, gained importance and has played a prominent role in the recent promotion of new industries, such as electric vehicles, and the buildup of related innovation ecosystems. With the MLP (2006), the "strategic emerging industries," and other innovation plans, the MOST started to manage, both directly and indirectly, a larger volume of resources. Seeking to address the problems of policy fragmentation and lack of coordination, S & T programs were reconfigured and grouped into fewer categories, with the objective of making R & D spending more effective. As Stephanie Christmann-Budian, an innovation expert from the Max Planck Institute for the History of Science, remarks: "Driven by dissatisfaction with earlier science policies, measures such as the reorganization of research funding in the mid-2010s, including the attempt to professionalize the administrative processes of research funding, build on an evaluation of earlier experiences ... there is clearly an awareness of looming problems, and a proactive stance toward solving these, leading to constant policy reformulation" (Interview #26; see also Christmann-Budian, 2012). Indeed, by the mid-2010s, a ministerial-level committee with the aim of overseeing S & T programs and funding, the Inter-Ministerial Joint Committee (IMJC), was initiated. The IMJC brings together the MOST, the Ministry of Finance (MOF), the NDRC, and other related ministries. The rise of the MOST contrasts with the experiences of other middle-income countries such as Vietnam. Despite the official rhetoric of promoting innovation and the identification of China's S & T policies as a role model, the Vietnamese MOST never reached the status of its Chinese counterpart (Klingler-Vidra & Wade, 2020; for comparisons with earlier East Asian developmental states, see Haggard, 2018: 35–39).

In addition, a new ministry was created in 2008 as a successor to the Ministry of Information Industry: the Ministry of Industry and Information Technology (MIIT). The MIIT soon became crucial in articulating technological upgrading policies. In contrast to the NDRC with its generalist profile, MIIT staff more closely resembled a technocratic ideal type. Initially, staff were mainly former managers of high-tech SOEs or were recruited from other state agencies with a focus on information technology (Wang, 2019). The MIIT quickly became instrumental in the design of sector-specific industrial policies, promoting "strategic emerging industries" and emphasizing ideas such as "leapfrog development." The innovation paradigm had thus found expression in a new bureaucratic body and the MIIT henceforth vied for policy authority.

Notably, the importance and influence of these agencies varies considerably between industries. While in some sectors they have learned to work together quite effectively, as we shall see in Section 3, in the traditional automotive sector, for example, the MIIT and the NDRC competed in the formulation of regulatory policies (Heilmann, 2017: 347). In the case of the photovoltaic industry, multiple central state agencies proposed different policy agendas, often developed independently from each other, thus undermining state capacity to regulate the industry (Chen, 2016). Therefore, despite improved bureaucratic coherence, problems of overall coordination and horizontal unity endure. Science and technology budgets, for example, are largely controlled by the MOF, but other ministries participating in the IMJC have similar authority, meaning that national-level coordination remains contested.[24] This

---

[24] Another "super ministry" established in the period is the Ministry of Human Resources and Social Security (MoHRSS), which oversees occupational standards, technical training, and skill

situation, however, cannot be equated with countries such as Vietnam, where "weak inter-ministerial coordination" is severely hampering the domestic innovation push (Klingler-Vidra & Wade, 2020: 727), or Latin American economies, where ministries often "work in silos with no coordination among them" (Paus, 2020: 675).

After 2013, this setup was complemented by the CCP's attempts to increase its control within the state, and more systematically utilize its regulatory capacity and consensus-building function. This involved creating or strengthening parallel advisory and decision-making party committees, known as "Leading Small Groups" (LSGs). Governmental entities did not completely lose their power, however. In fact, the same people are involved in formulating policy plans in the majority of fields, albeit in different capacities (Interviews #27, #28, #32). To date, the consequences of these changes unfortunately remain understudied, including the role of top-level LSGs, and this is therefore an area deserving of more scrutiny in the future – a daunting task given the major data collection challenges (for previous reports, see Miller, 2014; Johnson et al., 2017).

The CCP has undertaken several measures with the aim of improving the meritocratic recruitment and professional evaluation of bureaucrats. In 2006, a new Civil Service Law (CSL), in the pipeline for years, was finally approved; this expanded the definition of the category of "state civil servants." Essentially, the CSL aimed to integrate the state civil service system with party cadre personnel management, and, moving beyond the 1993 regulations, granted party committees and their Organizational Departments the authority to manage state officials, providing greater leverage over the state bureaucracy (Chan & Li, 2007). In sum, the CSL turned the principle of "the party manages cadres" into law (Burns & Wang, 2010) with the aim of securing greater control over the bureaucracy.[25]

The CSL also contributed to professionalizing the recruitment and evaluation of bureaucrats, thereby consolidating measures introduced with the 1993 regulations. Specific monitoring elements were reinforced, including audits and peer evaluation exercises, as a means of promotion for bureaucrats (Burns & Wang, 2010). Significantly, entering the civil service has become more competitive over the years. The ratio of applicants to civil service jobs surged from around

---

certification for the entire workforce. In the case of skill formation, however, it does not cooperate effectively with the Ministry of Education (Müller, 2017).

[25] Other administrative reforms were also meant to improve monitoring capabilities. The MOF, for instance, banned the practice of individual governmental units creating bank accounts at their own discretion and centralized existing accounts. These reforms allowed the central government to monitor financial transactions within the bureaucracy more easily and execute budgetary plans more swiftly (Ang, 2020).

ten applicants per position in 1994 to fifty-seven in 2014 (Heilmann, 2017). Data reveals that, after a decrease in the ratio from 2014 to 2017 and during the COVID-19 pandemic, it increased to sixty-five applicants per position in 2022 (see the online supplementary materials).

These measures, however, had limits. While the promotion of leading officials is often linked to their performance on economic targets (Li & Zhou, 2005), this mainly relates to higher levels of the administration.[26] Below that, cadres have much more limited chances of promotion, as Kostka & Yu (2015) reveal for county-level cadres. The vast majority of state employees are rank-and-file officers and street-level bureaucrats (Ang, 2020). This group's chances of upward mobility are slim. For them, incentives must come solely in the form of material benefits, such as bonuses and other fringe benefits, because their salaries are low. Moreover, the CSL does not eliminate collusion between local agents – in this case, supervisors and their subordinates. Many performance evaluations are merely pro forma, with over 99 percent of all civil servants sometimes being rated "outstanding" or "competent," qualifying them for bonuses and pay rises. Because supervisors are also evaluated by their subordinates through a system of peer evaluation, the continued existence of personal networks is unsurprising. Lastly, the CSL did not establish a civil service job protection regulation and therefore does not guarantee lifelong tenure, ideally immune from external interference (see also Zhou, 2010; Smith, 2015).

When Xi Jinping took power in early 2013 there was still a widespread perception of rampant corruption, especially at top level. The party-state initiated an anti-corruption campaign that went far beyond those launched by previous administrations in scope, intensity, and duration. It was reinforced by bureaucratic restructuring: the Central Discipline Inspection Commission (CDIC) played a key role and numerous Central Inspection Groups inspected state agencies, party organs, and research institutions. In 2017, several agencies were merged to create the National Supervisory Commission, which has considerable scope to conduct anti-corruption activities. While it is difficult to objectively assess the effectiveness of the campaign (Wedeman, 2020), it instilled fear in local bureaucrats, raising the question of whether it also had the (undesired) effect of dismantling local state–business coalitions, a question we will scrutinize in Section 2.2.3.

In the S & T system, researchers and technical staff have played an increasingly important role since the 2000s in policymaking, the buildup of local innovation infrastructures, and collaborating with business (also see Fu et al., 2022).

---

[26] Shih et al. (2012) provide a complementary explanation, arguing that promotions could be better explained as resulting from factional politics rather than just economic performance.

At the same time, their activities have also encountered limits. The performance evaluation system has provided powerful incentives to fulfill targets related to innovation, as attested by the rising number of patent applications (see Figure 5). A number of regulations have been enacted to boost incentives for patent filing, including the subsidization of the patent-filing process, patent-filing quotas for researchers, and direct rewards and promotion for filing patents (Schmid & Wang, 2017). Nevertheless, these measures attached excessive importance to quantitative outcomes rather than more fine-grained qualitative criteria (Fu, 2015; Appelbaum et al., 2018, Han & Appelbaum, 2018). Relatedly, evaluations are fast-paced – conducted annually or at even more frequent intervals – creating pressure to meet targets in the short term. As a result, researchers end up prioritizing quantity over quality in order to satisfy evaluation targets, which was also reflected in the proportion of experimental development investments in relation to basic research investments, and of utility or design patents compared with invention patents. Moreover, personal relations with cadres are still important for acquiring funds and securing support for research programs, leading to cases of fraud (Suttmeier, 2020).

The role of certain nongovernmental professional organizations, think tanks, and business forums such as the "China EV100" for the electric vehicle industry (Interview #32) was also strengthened by the 2010s. The China Association for Science and Technology (CAST), for instance, brings together scientists, engineers, and other professionals to "stimulate independent innovation." During this period, CAST's technical expertise and ability to provide analyses and evaluations improved. However, as it is formally subordinate to the CCP, it is unlikely that it will achieve significant autonomy from politics, perhaps undermining the chance of it providing truly independent policy advice (Cao & Suttmeier, 2017; Suttmeier, 2020).

In sum, targeted bureaucratic reforms were conducted to foster innovation-related goals. Efforts to improve national-level coordination were a top priority, and key agencies such as the NDRC, MIIT, and MOST became increasingly important. While the long-term goal of promoting innovation was widely acknowledged, and attempts were made to enforce policies through coherent "top-level design," legacies from the past – especially policy fragmentation and bureaucratic competition – still exist, and to a greater extent than in the canonical developmental states. Moreover, there were advances regarding the professional recruitment of bureaucrats, and S & T staff gained importance. Although patronage and political interference in the working of the bureaucracy has never been eradicated, it is now less susceptible to the kind of patrimonial relations that prevail in many low- and middle-income countries.

2.2.3 Difficulties in Forging Vertical Bureaucratic Coherence

To assess China's innovation activities, it is necessary to analyze vertical bureaucratic coherence as well. Here, we examine efforts undertaken within the systems of fiscal decentralization and cadre evaluation, as well as further administrative measures to make local bureaucrats work in tandem with central innovation objectives.

As noted in Section 2.1, central–local relations in the reform period were characterized by political centralization, far-reaching administrative decentralization, and a mismatch between fiscal revenue and expenditure mandates. The overarching goal of GDP growth led to implementation gaps and systematic cases of noncompliance with respect to policies which did not promise to boost local fiscal revenues quickly. While it is convenient for the center to use local governments as scapegoats for poor outcomes in policy implementation and, conversely, to portray itself as solving long-standing structural problems by wrestling against unruly local governments (Yang & Yan, 2018), this problem can actually be understood as a result of persistent inconsistencies in the central apparatus itself. First, the system of fiscal decentralization essentially concentrates revenues at the central level, thereby failing to provide the wherewithal for local governments to implement various policies. Second, the cadre evaluation system often advances multiple goals, resulting in conflicting policies. For example, in some contexts, the goal of increasing industrial profits required the dismissal of "redundant" workers, which in turn undermined the achievement of another goal, the maintenance of public order (Whiting, 2004).

Despite the increased importance of the central bureaucracy in fostering innovation, local governments continue to play a fundamental role – for example, by establishing regional innovation infrastructures, high-tech zones, specialized industrial clusters, science parks, and innovation platforms, especially in wealthier areas. The aforementioned fiscal mismatch, however, remains a feature of the system. In 2020, around 86 percent of budgetary expenditures were shouldered by subnational governments, while they accrued only 54 percent of budgetary revenues (NBS, 2020a). In fact, as depicted in Figure 6, not only are the subnational governments responsible for the vast majority of budgetary expenditures, they also spend more on S & T than the central government. For example, industrial guidance funds, a key instrument for funding the innovation drive, are mostly controlled by local governments with city governments accounting for almost twice as much funding as the center (Naughton, 2021: 107). Gao et al. (2021) find that R & D subsidies managed by local bureaucrats are more likely to encourage firms to promote innovative activities than those managed by central government. This is due to

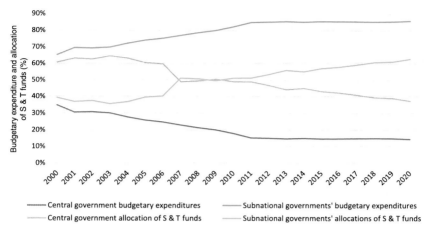

Figure 6 Budgetary expenditures and allocation of S & T funds: Central and subnational level (percentage of the total), 2000–2020

Source: Authors' elaboration with data from NBS (2020a, 2020b).

local governments' higher flexibility in managing programs, which gives recipient firms more leeway to deal with the inherent uncertainties of the innovation process. Given the unresolved fiscal mismatch, however, local governments still have a short-term orientation and a focus on chasing quick fiscal revenues. Hence, many of the S & T programs geared toward more long-term development are disadvantaged (Sun & Cao, 2021).

As part of the endeavor to better steer local bureaucrats in accordance with goals set by the center, a series of administrative measures, including but not limited to the cadre evaluation system, were implemented. Three important changes are worth emphasizing: first, local bureaucrats were subjected to an increasingly tight monitoring system which reduced their leeway, especially after Xi came to power; second, changes in the PRC's vertical administrative hierarchy were implemented to enhance the reach of the central state down to the local level(s); and third, local officials are now evaluated according to an even broader array of targets, especially related to innovation goals.

With regard to the first change, namely, measures to tighten the monitoring system, bonuses to reward local officials for attracting investment were prohibited in 2013 (Oi, 2020). Additionally, to curb state capture local bureaucrats were not allowed to hire professionals from businesses and social organizations for part-time government positions. These measures were to be enforced by the now powerful CDIC. Moreover, in 2015, local governments were ordered to detach themselves from LGFVs. As mentioned in Section 2.1.2, LGFVs were at the center of the "growth by any means" phase. The rationale behind these measures is clear. The central bureaucracy wants to make local bureaucrats comply with central directives. It also aims to curb corruption and address the population's discontent over the myriad shady deals at the local level. Use of LGFVs and the related accumulation of local debt resulted in escalating real estate prices and occasional protests over the misappropriation of peasant land (Wei, 2015; Su & Tao, 2017).

Despite the commendable goals, reduced leeway for local bureaucrats may stifle state–business ties, as some interviewees (Interviews #9, #22) and discussions with our informants on the mainland suggest. Anecdotal evidence alludes to local officials becoming more risk averse, and to entrepreneurs being less inclined to rely on their "privileged access" networks (Ang, 2020). Not only do these measures risk undermining the otherwise powerful incentives driving local governments; they may also be an ineffective way of steering bureaucrats toward innovation targets. The key issue is how to provide local governments with the wherewithal to finance their local expenditures. As the fiscal mismatch remains unresolved, officials are likely to continue trying to raise funds through alternative means – often those that provide quick and certain revenues, which can be at odds with the long-term and uncertain nature of innovation.

Second, another change has been a series of measures to streamline the multilayered vertical administrative structure, which frequently caused friction between different government levels. For example, the "province-leading county" system enacted in this period had the objective of empowering provinces so that they could bypass the prefectural level and reach the county level more effectively (Chung, 2015; Li & Yang, 2015; Donaldson, 2017).[27] More recently, under Xi Jinping, village cadres were formally incorporated into the party apparatus and hence are now fully subject to party rules, increasing the party's clout at the grassroots level (Wang & Mou, 2021). The rationale is to improve the control of the center over lower-level units, either by circumventing the administrative layers between them, or by reaching lower units more effectively.

Third, this period witnessed the diversification of targets for cadre evaluations. In line with the innovation paradigm, targets such as patent applications, the number and total output of high-tech companies, and exports of high-tech products came to the fore (Chen, 2017), as did increased emphasis on the quality of educational institutions (Postiglione, 2020).[28] The diversification of targets

---

[27] With the objective of combating local protectionism, bureaucratic units were already partly centralized in the late 1990s in a process Mertha (2005) describes as "soft centralization." This took place at the grassroots level, that is, township and county bureaucracies were recentralized up to the provincial level.

[28] The central government also diversified targets in other areas, such as public administration and social policy (Teets, 2015; Göbel & Heberer, 2017). The "growth by any means" period had seen

away from the focus on GDP growth was meant to change local behavior. However, the simultaneous drive toward reduced leeway for local bureaucrats has created gray areas regarding the type of behavior that is expected, encouraged, tolerable, or even undesirable. Conflicting goals have always existed (Whiting, 2004), but they have become more significant with the relativization of the primacy of GDP growth (Ang, 2020). The combination of contradictory targets and stricter central monitoring creates ambiguous incentives for local officials, with reports indicating cases ranging from blind compliance to local officials continuing to manipulate information to "game" the system (Wong, 2021; see also Zhang, 2017).

A related example typifying the ambiguous role local governments play is the creation of science parks, an area in which they have been proactive. Similar to S & T staff, local authorities end up prioritizing quantitative improvement in order to satisfy evaluation targets. Notably, many new science parks are found to be less productive than earlier ones (Yang & Lee, 2021). In the same vein, local authorities continue to promote the quick commercialization of adapted products and neglect investing in basic research (see Figure 4; for an example of such detrimental dynamics in nanotechnology, see Appelbaum et al., 2016).[29] According to Qiang Zhi, a leading Chinese expert in public administration and innovation, such short-termism is connected to the fact that "local officials typically plan no more than three or five years, in contrast to national bureaucrats who frequently have a time horizon of twenty years" (Interview #30).

Another ambiguity relates to how local bureaucrats engage with foreign capital (FDI) and how they balance the goals of indigenous innovation and local growth. In the case of the flat panel industry, Chen & Ku (2014) conclude that, while the central government was pushing for indigenously owned technologies, local governments were reluctant to sponsor domestic companies because their technologies were typically inferior to those produced by foreign firms, which potentially jeopardized the competitiveness of local industries. In the case of solar panels and wind turbines, Nahm (2017) shows that local governments supported domestic companies, while at the same time engaging with foreign firms in other segments of the value chain. In the end, although domestic firms did not become fully independent from foreign technology, they did achieve some technological upgrading (see Heilmann et al., 2013 for more evidence of the positive role of local experimentation combined with foreign capital; similar issues are discussed in Section 3).

---

less progress in social policy, as the latter's distributive nature rendered it less attractive than potentially lucrative experiments in the field of economic development.

[29] Note that in 2021, there was a new round of investment in basic research, the effects of which are yet to materialize (Interview #12).

While there is a strong sense in Western discourse that central–local relations have changed dramatically since Xi's rise to power, this perception contrasts with the substantial continuity observed in practice in the fields under scrutiny. China remains politically centralized but administratively decentralized, and the fiscal mismatch inherited from the 1990s has not been addressed. In relation to industrial and innovation policies, local governments continue to experiment, as our fieldwork on innovation platforms and the promotion of electric vehicles indicates (see Section 3; Interviews #4, #5, #7, #11, #12, #22, #24). This should not come as a surprise, as experimentation in these domains has the potential to benefit powerful local elites. The recent tightening of the monitoring system does not preclude experimentation in priority areas selected by the central leadership (see Heffer & Schubert, 2023). Rather than seeing an abrupt end to local experimentation, the period has been marked by attempts to shift experimentation toward innovation goals. This demanded a similar reorientation of state–business coalitions, a topic that we will now scrutinize.

2.2.4 Coalitions and the Increasing Importance of Consultative and Disciplining Mechanisms

In this section, we analyze the extent to which the bureaucracy has been able to better promote information exchange with business and between science and industry. Furthermore, we consider attempts to discipline domestic businesses and push them toward meeting innovation goals, mechanisms which were largely unheard of in the 1980s and 1990s.

As discussed, local state–business coalitions before the 2000s were underpinned by the party-state providing space for many business sectors to gradually emerge, for private ownership to become legitimate, for a number of business associations (BAs) to develop, and for researchers and technical staff to operate in the market realm. The literature concurs that businesses and their numerous associations started to use a wide range of channels to lobby the state, mostly at local level (Deng & Kennedy, 2010; Teets, 2013; Heberer & Schubert, 2019; Shen et al., 2020). This, however, was not a one-way street. Bureaucrats also had an interest in working closely with business. In particular – and against the background of the growing significance of innovation and industrial policies from the 2000s onward – the need to obtain relevant and sector-specific information from businesses and their associations increased.

While personalized and reciprocal connections (*guanxi*) were (and still are) very relevant, institutionalized consultative bodies grew in importance – from local BAs and chambers of commerce to large federations such as the All-China Federation of Industry and Commerce (ACFIC), local and national consultative legislative bodies such as the Chinese People's Political Consultative Conference (CPPCC), People's Congresses, and ministries (Deng & Kennedy, 2010; ten Brink, 2019). Notably, there has been a renewed interest in studying institutions such as the CPPCC as possible arenas of interaction between bureaucrats and entrepreneurs (Tsang, 2009; Sun et al., 2014, Chen, 2015; Sagild & Ahlers, 2019). Although these consultative bodies provide very limited room for political inclusion and citizen participation, they do function as mechanisms that enable information exchange and the articulation of entrepreneurs' interests. Sagild and Ahlers (2019) argue that the drafting of policy proposals – which can be done at any time throughout the year – is the main formal mechanism the CPPCC has to facilitate information exchange, and they note a rise in the number of proposals. Chen and Huang (2019) observe that many of these proposals stem from the countless business chambers which, facilitated by the ACFIC, forward them to the CPPCC. Since the 2000s, the ACFIC has gained better access to policymaking, and it often organizes the collective interests of entrepreneurs and local business chambers enabling them to submit proposals to the CPPCC, which in turn can pass these on to relevant governmental bodies. While welcomed and even encouraged by the party-state,[30] this is done within rigid political limits, ensuring it does not challenge the hegemony of the CCP (Tsang, 2009; Sagild & Ahlers, 2019).

Likewise, with regard to technology development, companies and research institutions have been encouraged to provide input into policy design. While some initiatives under the innovation paradigm resemble national-level research consortia, like those in Japan in the 1980s which brought together universities and industries to develop microchips, most are local level. Again, this is connected to the pivotal importance of local coalitions in a continental-sized economy. To improve the effectiveness of mechanisms to foster technology transfer between research institutes and companies, a new policy was enacted in 2016 which gave academics more opportunities to work part-time in enterprises. Moreover, inventors themselves are now allowed to retain a greater share of the income accrued from the commercialization of products that use intellectual property developed by scientists and research institutes (Cao & Suttmeier, 2017; Interviews #21, #30). This illustrates that, even with the general tightening of party-state monitoring, some segments of Chinese society – those instrumental in implementing the innovation-driven strategy – can actually operate in a more relaxed, business-friendly environment. Rather than conducting a full-blown and indiscriminate attack on agents' leeway, the

---

[30] This was recently reemphasized by the State Council, which urged governments at all levels to take inputs from enterprises, BAs, and chambers of commerce into consideration when formulating new regulations (State Council, 2019).

ruling elite seems to be selectively adjusting what is encouraged and what is prohibited.

Relatedly, more scientists have been integrated into local coalitions since the 2000s. This is a response to the difficulties of translating fundamental basic or even applied science into commercial innovations – the proverbial "Valley of Death." Research institutes of the CAS, for instance, only recently began to make progress in transferring scientific and technological knowledge to industry, despite the success of CAS reforms in terms of scientific performance more generally (Zhang et al., 2019). To further address this problem, a diverse set of innovation intermediaries supported by the government – known as "innovation platforms" (*chuangxin pingtai*) – have been created. These platforms aim to foster local science–industry collaboration and match technological specifications to firm capabilities (Armanios & Eesley, 2021; see Fan & Li, 2022 and Yu et al., 2020 for recent discussions among CAS academics on the need to further reform research institutions and use "market mechanisms" to improve commercialization).

A series of organization-building policy initiatives has led to the strengthening of research institutions, both within firms and beyond. One such initiative is related to attaining the status of a "New R & D Institute" (*xinxing yanfa jigou*). This program has gained momentum, especially since 2015 (Conlé et al., 2021). While anecdotal evidence from fieldwork suggests that certain New R & D Institutes are not running smoothly, some are actually quite effective. These organizations have proven capable of facilitating different forms of knowledge transfer to close gaps between the science system and local businesses, although they still mainly stimulate firms' adaptive capacities and incremental or "new-to-the-firm" innovation. Moreover, the need to improve weak knowledge infrastructures in manufacturing hotspots such as the Pearl River Delta has become critical. Until the early 2000s, major universities and renowned research institutes were still mainly located in just a few cities, Beijing in particular, and were thus separated from most manufacturing centers. Since then, local governments have attracted nonlocal universities and CAS institutes, as well as establishing their own research institutions. Shenzhen was particularly successful in this respect, hosting, for instance, the Shenzhen Institute of Advanced Technology, a CAS institute which performs very strongly in transnational patent applications, and a New R&D Institute established by the genomics company BGI Shenzhen (Conlé et al., 2021; Conlé et al., 2023).

In parallel with the emphasis on innovation-related targets for local officials, central policymakers have encouraged businesses to invest more in innovative activities. The innovation paradigm thus found a clear counterpart in policies for business and S & T staff. The latter have benefited not only from more mechanisms of consultation with state officials, but also easier access to public funds for this purpose. After experimenting with subsidies such as the initially poorly coordinated R & D tax credit policy, the policy was extended nationwide in 2008. It provides tax deductions for firms with high-tech status and has, overall, been found to increase patents and investments in R & D, especially in manufacturing and for large companies (Chen & Yang, 2019; Gao et al., 2021; Boeing et al., 2022). In 2016, the criteria for companies to be classified as high-tech were relaxed further, with the aim of incentivizing more enterprises, especially small and medium-sized companies, to become more innovative (Liu et al., 2017).[31] This of course leads to concerns about state capture and the misuse of public resources, which, from the developmental state perspective, brings the importance of disciplining mechanisms to the fore.

The central bureaucracy has adjusted its policy to discipline recipients of R & D subsidies. While the state's expectations from business – more investment in innovative activities – became clearer, these are still broad categories and allow businesses to use state resources for different ends, whether legally or illegally. For example, high-tech firms have been found to seek this classification status due to the easy access to government funds it provides, rather than an interest in pursuing innovative endeavors. There are also cases of firms distorting their financial and patent figures to become eligible for R & D subsidies, especially at the local level (Liu et al., 2017; Sun & Cao, 2021). Moreover, some R & D subsidies have ended up being used by industries that are not prioritized in the innovation push, such as real estate, catering services, and entertainment (Chen & Yang, 2019; Boeing et al., 2022). The state thus needs to make sure not only that the allocation of funds is tied to monitorable targets, but that the achievement of these targets is not manipulated by business.

Seeking to address these issues, a policy adjustment (MOF, 2015) was announced in 2015 with the objective of prohibiting R & D subsidies in industries such as real estate, catering services, and entertainment, thereby tailoring funding to more innovative sectors (Chen & Yang, 2019). Following a similar logic, the MIIT created the "Little Giants" (*xiao juren*) program in 2018, in which small and medium-sized enterprises (SMEs), specialized in niche manufacturing segments such as high-end equipment, new energy, and new materials, would receive favorable treatment in the form of tax breaks and access to domestic capital markets. Crucially, the criteria for being classified as a Little Giant includes a minimum number of valid invention patents and investment in R & D (Cortese, 2022; Hui, 2022). This is clearly intended to

---

[31] High-tech companies are also eligible for land subsidies and are often privileged in public procurement regulations (Liu et al., 2017).

channel investments into potentially innovative companies in priority sectors, thus guiding the sectoral profile of investments of the economy.[32] It is also related to the more recent "crackdown" on businesses that started in mid-2021. The sectors targeted in this campaign were mostly those that are not characterized by strong technological upgrading prospects, ranging from financial services to gaming and real estate,[33] while manufacturing sectors – traditional and high-tech alike – have mostly been spared. Consumer internet giants such as Baidu, Alibaba, and Tencent were forced to realign their business models with the bureaucracy's overriding goals and, interestingly enough, all have announced increased investment into chipmaking and cloud computing (Cortese, 2022). In fact, as we shall see in Section 3, manufacturing sectors continue to receive generous support from the state.

In 2022, the central bureaucracy also announced plans to terminate patent-filing subsidies to correct the distortion and fraud created by the system depicted in Section 2 (State Intellectual Property Office, 2022). While these subsidies and the inclusion of patents as an official target produced positive results (see Figure 5), eventually it became obvious that too many agents were manipulating the system. Moreover, the MOF (2015) policy document excludes simple product modifications or duplications from eligibility for R & D tax deductions, which constitutes an adjustment to previous policies and indicates bureaucratic learning, this time related to China's disciplining mechanisms. Instead of trialing some rigid "best practice" recommendation, bureaucratic action seems to be constantly adapting.

The tightening of the monitoring system, anti-corruption measures, and the reforms we have analyzed certainly did not put an end to the misuse of public funds, but they significantly altered the dominant types of corruption. As Ang (2020) has shown, cases of outright embezzlement and theft of public funds – the forms of corruption most harmful to economic development – have indeed fallen dramatically since the early 2000s. The type that has become prevalent, in the meantime, is a form of "access money," characterized not by outright theft, but by the exchange of benefits between bureaucrats and businessmen. Here, the latter spend money – legally or illegally – to get privileged access to valuable assets such as land, loans, and subsidies, while the former receive bribes. Notably, this type of nontransparent coalition-building may facilitate, rather than harm, productive investment (Ang, 2020; see May et al., 2019 for a comparison with India and Brazil).

---

[32] The inspiration for the program is Germany's "hidden champions", that is, successful SMEs, thus indicating the bureaucracy's attentiveness to foreign experiences.

[33] This is related to attempts at curtailing speculative investment, the danger of "abandoning the real for the virtual" (*tuoshi xiangxu*), and to instead focus on productive activities.

The ability to introduce new measures to discipline business and to change course more generally – more of which is described in Section 3 – is tied to the unique distribution of power between state and business. In comparison to other emerging capitalist economies, the party-state has stronger political capabilities to implement disciplining mechanisms and, on balance, maintains the upper hand over business and has effective tools of legal repression at its disposal (Zhang, 2019; but see Rithmire & Chen, 2021 on relations between large private firms and political elites characterized by "mutual endangerment").

Under Xi Jinping, the CCP itself has assumed a greater role in controlling and managing entrepreneurs, BAs, and science organizations (Shen et al., 2020; Suttmeier, 2020). For instance, the increasing penetration of private companies by party cells further empowers the party-state by facilitating the transmission of information (Grünberg & Drinhausen, 2019; for a recent analysis of SOE governance, see Leutert & Eaton, 2021). Furthermore, following a co-optation strategy, the party seeks to recruit BA leaders as party branch secretaries while, at the same time, BAs retain some functional autonomy (Shen et al., 2020). These developments confirm the continuing existence of close coalitions between economic and political elites, where entrepreneurs and BAs have considerable scope for business operations, albeit within the political limits set, tacitly or explicitly, by the party-state. What has changed since the "growth by any means" period is the growing importance of mechanisms of consultation between bureaucrats, businesses, and scientists, which are pivotal for the exchange of industry-specific information and technology transfer, as well as the continuous adjustments of disciplining mechanisms – the limits of which we will discuss in the next section.

Two additional factors help to explain the continued relative political weakness of entrepreneurs and thus their dependency on the party-state. First, while responsible for the bulk of the growth, the private sector is composed mostly of SMEs. The largest Chinese corporations, measured by total assets or sales, are actually state-owned, eclipsing private or semi-private firms such as Alibaba, Tencent, and Midea (Sutherland & Ning, 2015). Second, the importance of foreign capital, especially in high-tech sectors, diminishes the political power of domestic entrepreneurs. Foreign enterprises still play a much larger role than in the East Asian developmental states (Liu & Tsai, 2021), and have crafted coalitions with local bureaucrats, especially with local departments of international commerce (Chen, 2017, 2018). These limitations on the power of entrepreneurs should not necessarily come as a surprise. Some decades ago, Shue (1994) argued that Deng Xiaoping's measures of granting a greater role to the market and to the lower levels of the bureaucracy have always been the means, but never the end, of the reformist program. In this sense, China's national ruling elite is less vulnerable politically and can therefore afford to adjust its mechanisms of disciplining business more than many other middle-income countries.

3 Assessing Technological Upgrading: Semiconductors and Electric Vehicles

We now delve into two industries that have recently been heavily promoted: semiconductors and electric vehicles. In general, technological upgrading in these industries is found to be correlated with increased bureaucratic coherence, which has strengthened capacities for policymaking and disciplining business as well as information sharing between bureaucrats, businessmen, and scientists. At the same time, we highlight flaws and demonstrate that advances in the field of electric vehicles have been more successful than those in the field of semiconductors. These varied results can be explained by an interplay of technological and market structure characteristics and bureaucratic factors. As a new industry in the making, barriers to entry are lower for electric vehicles and dominant business models are still being established worldwide. The semiconductor industry, however, is highly consolidated, with a few very large and well-established global players, increasing barriers to entry and technological catch-up costs. We find that China's system of decentralized governance and experimentation is more conducive to technological upgrading in emerging industries, such as electric vehicles, than for semiconductors, where a more centralized system capable of concentrating funds into a few big businesses would probably be more suitable. We also find that discipline over business proved to be more effective for electric vehicles than for semiconductors.

3.1 Semiconductors

Efforts to foster the integrated circuits semiconductor industry are intended to promote catch-up with global players and incumbent leaders in a technology field that is key for many sectors, ranging from IT products to artificial intelligence, autonomous vehicles, and military applications.[34] As a consolidated industry worldwide, there is already proven demand in the market, meaning latecomers like China can benefit from lower market uncertainty. The innovation paradigm places particular emphasis on the semiconductor industry, given its economic, military, and geopolitical importance. In this sense, China's

---

[34] Semiconductors can be divided into different types: memory, logic, micro, analogue, optoelectronics, discrete, and sensors. Integrated circuit semiconductors refer to the first four and make up the largest share of the industry.

prioritization of semiconductors is a good example of the role played by increased concerns about national security and, concomitantly, indigenous technology development.

When compared with other middle-income countries, the recent development of China's semiconductor industry is remarkable. However, dependence on foreign technology is still enormous, and Chinese actors do not control crucial intellectual property in the value chain (Grimes & Du, 2022). As a result, China does not challenge the hegemony of dominant players in the industry. The heightened geopolitical conflict between China and the United States, with the latter strengthening its export restrictions, has certainly hampered China's efforts to upgrade in this industry.

Let us examine this more closely. The value chain of the semiconductor industry can be divided into three segments: design, fabrication or manufacturing, and assembly or testing and packaging. The first segment, design, is skills intensive and requires high R & D expenditure. The fabrication segment is very capital intensive, due to the large and expensive facilities and equipment it requires, and also demands significant R & D expenditure. In contrast, assembly is more labor intensive and characterized by lower technological requirements and thin profit margins. While design and fabrication concentrate on the higher value-added steps of the chain, assembly concentrates on the lower value-added steps (Fuller, 2016; Kleinhans & Baisakova, 2020). Other core inputs for the value chain include electronic design automation (EDA) tools – software, hardware, and services to write the design code – and fabrication capital equipment, key inputs for manufacturing. An additional criterion can be used to assess the degree of technological upgrading: the process node, typically measured in nanometers (nm). Other things being equal, the smaller the process node, the more advanced the technology. We will now assess how the central bureaucracy has attempted to promote the industry and the problems it faced in doing so.

3.1.1 Increased Central Bureaucratic Coherence, but Limited Industry Progress

The PRC has a long history of promoting the semiconductor industry, going back to the 1960s. In the 1990s, ambitions were revived by drawing on a combination of SOEs and joint ventures. These attempts, however, did not yield significant results (Fuller, 2016). In 2000, the state granted further, albeit rather tentative, support in the form of tax breaks and selected import duty exemptions. The total resources committed to the industry were limited, and as Fuller (2019: 269) remarks, "by 2004, subsidy payments amounted to only

200 million RMB, an amount equivalent to only 0.3 percent of China's total 2004 domestic IC [integrated circuit] production." As in other industries, by the early 2000s China was heavily dependent on foreign technology, its policies did not produce any relevant technological upgrading by local firms, and there was a lack of policy consistency.

With the emerging innovation paradigm, the industry gained momentum and a renewed and more decisive push was initiated. The long-term plan, "MLP 2006," already contained directives for the promotion of the industry, but it was some years before the bureaucracy formulated more specific policies. In 2011, more tax breaks were offered – this time of greater magnitude. Finally, in 2014, an industry-specific program was formulated, the "National Integrated Circuit Industry Development Outline," launched by the State Council. Since then, the PRC has made the development of semiconductors a top priority. In order to finance this massive effort, a state-backed investment fund (known as the "Big Fund"), overseen by the MIIT and MOF (Pan et al., 2021), was also launched and is estimated to have raised almost 140 billion RMB by the end of 2019, when its first phase was concluded. The second phase began shortly afterwards, with a registered capital of over 200 billion RMB. Several other policy documents followed, mostly issued by the State Council, but also by the NDRC and the MOF.[35] Moreover, the MOST had already created a program to support IC design, selecting a total of eight pilot cities for this purpose, and offered inputs for the design firms that were springing up at the time. With the objective of strengthening national coordination of the myriad policies and ministries involved, a LSG for the industry was created in 2014 to steer national minister-ial-level agencies (Lee & Kleinhans, 2021). All these efforts indicate attempts to increase bureaucratic coherence and policy consistency, in comparison with the previous era.

In 2014, some of the main goals of the new push included developing the capacity to manufacture 14/16 nm chips, having internationally competitive fabrication capital equipment by 2020, and meeting 40 percent of domestic chip consumption by 2020 and 70 percent by 2025. Since then, a substantial quanti-tative expansion of the industry has taken place, but the qualitative results deserve closer scrutiny. The total production value soared from around 6.6 billion US dollars in the mid-2000s to over 80 billion US dollars by 2018 (Fuller, 2019). Nevertheless, this expansion was mostly based on assembly and design, despite progress in fabrication (Kleinhans & Baisakova, 2020; Interview #16). By 2019, the labor-intensive, low value-added assembly

---

[35] See Duchâtel (2021: 41) and Lee and Kleinhans (2021: 64) for a list of the most relevant policy documents.

segment accounted for 31.1 percent of China's total revenues in the industry, while the global average was only 14 percent (SBIIT, 2021).[36]

The design segment accounted for 40.5 percent of China's total revenues, while the global average was 29.5 percent (SBIIT, 2021). Notably, a truly global player operating at the technological frontier emerged: Shenzhen-based HiSilicon. However, HiSilicon is still dependent on the internal purchases of its parent corporation, Huawei, and seems to have developed largely independently of the national policies launched in 2014 (Fuller, 2019). That said, Huawei has benefited tremendously from state policies aimed at upgrading its technological capabilities – in the form of tax breaks, grants, subsidized bank loans, and subsidized land for research facilities, for instance (Ezell, 2021). In this sense, HiSilicon's success can be partly attributed to state efforts, albeit indirectly.

In fabrication, revenues accounted for 28.4 percent of total revenues in the industry, while the global average, at 56.5 percent, was roughly twice as high (SBIIT, 2021). The two major companies are Huahong and SMIC. As the domestic technology leader, SMIC has gained control of a 14/16 nm process node technology, meeting the 2020 goal; yet industry leaders Samsung and TSMC (Taiwan) have mastered a 7 nm and 5 nm technology, respectively, and both are rapidly moving toward 3 nm. The position of SMIC clearly illustrates China's performance in the industry. On the one hand, it has achieved a status that no other comparable middle-income country has, not to mention advanced manufacturing powerhouses such as Germany; on the other, SMIC is a long way behind global leaders and the prospects of catching up are poor, according to industry experts (Interview #17). Table 1 depicts SMIC's continuous upgrading throughout the 2010s, revealing that it has almost managed to catch up with UMC – Taiwan's second largest manufacturer and the world's fourth largest, in 2019, by sales revenues (Kleinhans & Baisakova, 2020: 15). However, SMIC is clearly behind industry leader TSMC, which concentrates around 45 percent of its revenues in technology nodes that SMIC has not yet mastered.[37]

Finally, when it comes to EDA tools, no significant advances were made, the market being overwhelmingly dominated by US companies. In fabrication capital equipment, the situation is similar (Fuller, 2021; Grimes & Du, 2022).[38] The lack of progress in these two segments seriously limits the

[36] Global semiconductor production is concentrated in a few regions, especially in East Asia, the United States, and some European countries.
[37] Recently, industry watchers reported that SMIC is already capable of producing 7 nm chips, but on a very limited scale. Because this was achieved by employing older capital inputs, it probably entails lower production yields.
[38] The largest EDA companies, Cadence, Synopsys, and Mentor Graphics, originate from the United States, although the latter has been acquired by Siemens. For capital equipment, Japan (Canon and Nikon) and the Netherlands (ASML) play major roles.

Table 1 Sales revenue breakdown by technology node

	SMIC			UMC	TSMC
Technology node	**2010**	**2015**	**2020**	**2020**	**2020**
5 nm	–	–	–	–	8%
7 nm	–	–	–	–	34%
10 nm	–	–	–	–	1%
14–28 nm	–	–	9%	13%	30%
40–45 nm	–	16%	16%	23%	9%
55–65 nm	5%	24%	30%	17%	5%
90 nm	17%	4%	3%	11%	2%
130 nm	33%	11%	5%	11%	3%
180 nm	28%	42%	33%	13%	7%
350 nm	17%	3%	4%	11%	2%

Note: Data for UMC is the unweighted average of the four quarters of 2020. All other data is annual. Comparisons with Intel and Samsung are less relevant because these are not pure foundries, but integrated device manufacturers.

Source: SMIC (various years), TSMC (2020), and UMC (2020).

prospect of catching up with industry leaders. Nonetheless, mature technology nodes will enjoy strong demand in the foreseeable future. This gives Chinese companies the opportunity to thrive beyond high-end market segments. As industry stakeholders state, "it is under-appreciated how much opportunity there is in China that's not dependent on those very leading-edge capabilities" (cited in Slodkowski, 2022). Last but not least, the Chinese bureaucracy is increasingly willing to invest in new semiconductor materials, such as gallium nitride, which could allow companies to leapfrog incumbent firms, albeit with no guarantee of success (Lee, 2022).

3.1.2 Persistent Vertical Bureaucratic Incoherence

As discussed in Section 2, the existence of multiple targets coupled with a fiscal mismatch between revenues and expenditures shapes the behavior of local bureaucrats; this leads to a short-term orientation and the pursuit of quick fiscal revenues. Similar problems beset the semiconductor push. While local governments have launched region-specific five-year plans and set up regional investment funds, the existence of conflicting evaluation targets generates ambiguous results. Moreover, localities adopted differing promotion strategies, leading to regional variation in outcomes and dispersion of investments.

Promotion of local bureaucrats is still tied to the attraction of large-scale investment. But now, increased high-tech output, regardless of ownership, also matters in evaluations. Considering the competitive advantage of many foreign firms, it is no surprise that officials were eager to attract and support them (Fuller, 2019). In the 2000s, for example, the government of the coastal metropolis Suzhou established a plant for UMC (Taiwan) – and it is still the largest fabrication company there. Despite the "indigenous innovation" rhetoric and the top priority assigned to semiconductors, FDI and MNCs are still very relevant. In 2020, among the top five manufacturing companies operating in the PRC, measured by total revenues, only two, SMIC and Huahong, were Chinese (SBIIT, 2021).

The semiconductor push has led local governments to support new companies, even those with no previous experience, in a somewhat haphazard manner (Hille & Yu, 2020). Relatedly, there is considerable regional variation in the implementation of the push, often resulting from differences in inherited industrial structures and state–business interactions. Shanghai, for example, has an industrial structure where large state-controlled conglomerates dominate and are typically selected to implement central policies (Zhang, 2023). In other cities, like Shenzhen or Suzhou, the participation of SOEs is much lower, and, in the case of the latter, foreign capital is more dominant. Outcomes in terms of technological upgrading also vary dramatically. While cities like Shanghai or Shenzhen perform relatively well, traditional manufacturing hotspots, such as Suzhou or Dongguan, concentrate around 60 percent and 80 percent, respectively, of their total revenues in the low value-added assembly segment (Guangdong Department of Industry and Information Technology, 2016; SBIIT, 2021). This dispersion of investments throughout the country is particularly harmful for a mature industry characterized by large-scale investments and huge capital concentration. It denotes a substantial lack of policy coordination and duplication of investments – hallmarks of the "growth by any means" phase. A strategy based on concentrating investments in a few localities would probably be more appropriate, albeit highly challenging given the limitations of China's vertical bureaucratic coherence.

3.1.3 Coalitions and Weaker Disciplining Mechanisms

It should be no surprise that the Chinese government plays a significant role in the semiconductor industry, given that in other countries, too, the state has historically been involved in the rise of domestic companies.[39] Since the 2014

---

[39] In the early days of Silicon Valley, the US Department of Defense provided numerous contracts for local companies, thereby mitigating the risk of developing new technologies (Leslie, 2000). In Taiwan, when TSMC and UMC were created in the 1980s, the state contributed around 48 percent of total initial capital in each case (Wong, 2011: 23). State-backed research institutes

push, the bureaucracy not only steered the overall development strategy and provided funding, but also forged coalitions with businesses and scientists to promote the exchange of industry-specific information. Our empirical study of policy proposals from local CPPCCs in the cities of Shenzhen, Suzhou, and Dongguan during the 2015–20 period reveals intensive communication between local businesses, bureaucrats, and university representatives. Members of the CPPCCs from business or research institutions frequently advanced policy proposals regarding the need to invest more in R & D and innovation platforms – to promote better integration between universities and enterprises, to attract skilled workers and provide subsidies for training, to create better financing channels, and to encourage companies to purchase domestically produced semiconductors (see the online supplementary materials).

Business associations also serve as intermediaries in linking small and medium-sized companies to local universities, research institutes, and other high-tech firms (Zhang, 2023). Beyond BAs, innovation intermediaries, such as R & D consortia and the New R & D Institutes, are utilized to promote science–industry collaboration and match technological specifications to firm capabilities (Zhang, 2018; Conlé et al., 2021). One of the most sophisticated platforms, the Shanghai IC R&D Center, located in Zhangjiang High-Tech Park and adjacent to SMIC, Huahong, and Huali Microelectronics, has built an advanced development and equipment test platform.[40] In Shenzhen, state officials and a broad range of business actors developed closer and more enduring ties, closer supplier linkages, and a more intensive exchange of industry-specific information. This made it easier to commit firms "to strengthening their absorptive capacity and research skills" (Zhang, 2018: 326; see also Zhang, 2023). Early in the process, for instance, the Shenzhen IC Design base launched an MA in integrated circuits design in partnership with the Hong Kong University of Science and Technology to address the skilled labor shortage (SZICC, 2012). The same holds for the recently launched Southeast University's joint innovation center with HiSilicon, and the IC Scientific Research Talent Cooperation between Fudan University, Xidian University, and Huawei.

---

such as the Industrial Technology Research Institute (ITRI) also played a major role. The same holds for the Interuniversity Microelectronics Centre (IMEC) in Europe. Extreme ultraviolet lithography (EUV) technology was created, in part, by IMEC and has since been commercialized by the Dutch company ASML (which has also relied on subsidies from the Dutch government in the past). Extreme ultraviolet lithography enables producers to create cutting-edge chips smaller than 7 nm (The Economist, 2020, 2021).

[40] SMIC also collaborates with the CAS Institutes of Microelectronics and Microsystems, Fudan University, Zhejiang University, Peking University, and Tsinghua University regarding technology and patents as well as to address shortages of skilled labor.

Furthermore, in response to concerns about the stability of supply chains in strategic industries such as semiconductors during the US–China trade war, a new consultative mechanism was established, largely in coastal cities. This comprises the appointment of top city officials as industry-specific "supply chain chiefs" (*gongyinglian fuzeren*) and "supply chain owners" (*gongyinglian zhu*) – that is, company managers, directors of BAs, and industry experts – to better coordinate upgrading activities (Qu, 2021; see Interview #24). While it is too early to evaluate this experiment, one local informant explained that it may enable firms to "gradually acquire the right to speak and achieve leadership in the industrial chain through their own strength in market competition" (Interview #22).

However, close state–business ties also resulted in collusion, exemplified by unfit firms receiving public funds. Previous studies indicated that as bureaucrats often lacked the technical knowledge to judge whether a firm was actually succeeding in promoting technological upgrading, they could easily be fooled (Fuller, 2016). This once again highlights the need to strengthen disciplining mechanisms.

Notably, the classic disciplining mechanism identified by Amsden (1989) – using a clearly measurable and easily monitorable target, namely, export performance – does not play a major role in the PRC. Given the differences in geographical size between China and South Korea (or Taiwan), this is no surprise. Figure 7 depicts the share of total revenues for SMIC and TSMC accrued by customers headquartered abroad – a proxy for exports. Clearly, TSMC exported the vast majority of its production. SMIC, however, is much more inward oriented. Moreover, SMIC's share of exports has recently been on the decline. While this can be partially attributed to the "trade and tech war" since the late 2010s, the data reveals that lower participation in foreign markets is a structural trait. The same holds for other, less sophisticated, domestic firms.

Deprived of the option of using exports to discipline firms, the bureaucracy uses a series of measures and detailed regulations instead. This alternative is, however, more human-resource intensive and therefore more demanding than using exports, because bureaucrats need state-of-the-art technical knowledge and the commensurate capabilities to monitor and enforce policy implementation.[41]

Analyzing the main semiconductor-related policy documents of the past twenty years reveals how the use of Enterprise Income Tax (EIT) has been employed in order to both provide fiscal incentives for semiconductor

---

[41] In South Korea, the use of exports essentially reduced monitoring and disciplining costs for the bureaucracy. As a result, industrial policymaking in East Asia, "did not require sophisticated calculations and a highly skilled bureaucracy" (Wade, 2005: 100). On the contrary, sole reliance on a strengthened bureaucracy is much costlier.

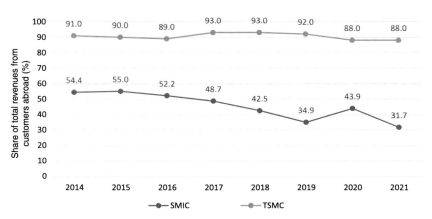

Figure 7 Share of total revenues from customers headquartered abroad
(percentage)

Note: Data for both companies is for the fourth quarter of each year. Data for SMIC was obtained by subtracting the revenues from products sold in China from the overall total. Data for TSMC was obtained by subtracting the revenues from products sold in the Asia-Pacific region from the overall total. As the Asia-Pacific region includes Taiwan and other countries, the data presented in the figure actually underestimates TSMC's share of exports.

Source: SMIC (various years) and TSMC (various years).

companies and progressively nudge companies to deliver more advanced products. Table 2 presents a comparison of EIT policies based on the relevant State Council (2000, 2011, 2020a) documents.[42]

The State Council (2000) introduced the "two exemptions and three half reductions" (*liang mian san jian ban*) policy, according to which companies were exempt from EIT for the first two years, and for the next three years paid only half the statutory rate. The State Council (2011) then built on this, but with modifications: first, the differentiated rates and regulations of EIT became a function of the companies' degree of technological sophistication, measured by the technology node. Hence, companies producing at 800 nm or less were subject to the same policy, but those which managed to produce at 250 nm or less, and which had been in operation for at least fifteen years, could benefit from a "five exemptions and five half reductions" (*wu mian wu jian ban*) policy: for the first five years companies would be exempt from EIT, and for the next five they would pay only half the statutory rate. Here, for the first time, an attempt to link the amount of fiscal support to the degree of technological sophistication is observed. The requirement of at least fifteen years of

---

[42] For further analysis of these documents, see Fuller (2016, 2021) and Sutter (2021).

Table 2 Disciplining mechanisms: EIT regulations

Policy document	2000 State Council (2000)	2011 State Council (2011)	2020 State Council (2020a)
EIT regulations	Software companies: "two exemptions and three half reductions." For other key software companies (determined by the central government), a reduced rate of 10%.	Companies producing at 800 nm or less: "two exemptions and three half reductions." Companies producing at 250 nm or less and in operation for over fifteen years: "five exemptions and five half reductions." For other companies, a reduced rate of 15%.	Companies producing at 130 nm or less and in operation for over ten years: "two exemptions and three half reductions." Companies producing at 65 nm or less and in operation for over fifteen years: "five exemptions and five half reductions." Companies producing at 28 nm or less and in operation for over fifteen years are exempt from EIT from the first to the tenth year.

Sources: State Council (2000, 2011, 2020a); Fuller (2016).

experience was also new, possibly aimed at excluding companies without proper know-how. The State Council (2020a) document continued to build on this logic, but now, in line with the development of the industry as a whole, it introduced tighter technological requirements: for companies producing at 130 nm or less and in operation for over ten years, the "two exemptions and three half reductions" policy applies. For companies producing at 65 nm or less, and in operation for over fifteen years, the "five exemptions and five half reductions" applies. Finally, companies producing at 28 nm or less, and in operation for over fifteen years, are exempt from EIT from the first to the tenth year. Progressively, then, the bureaucracy has been trying to use its tax and fiscal policies to discipline businesses.

Another source of discipline, also extensively used in South Korea and Taiwan, was the periodic rounds of rationalization or industry consolidation when too many firms had entered the market (Amsden, 1989; Wade, 1990). The two recent State Council (2011, 2020a) documents, contrary to the State Council (2000) document, explicitly encourage restructuring through mergers and acquisitions. However, with no binding regulation on this matter, prospects for industry consolidation and therefore more effective exploitation of economies of scale are undermined.

There has also been a gradual shift in the focus of these policy documents. While the 2000 document still referred to the "software industry" more generally, including semiconductors, the 2011 document has a more targeted focus on semiconductors. The 2020 document continued this, adding a specific focus on capital equipment, EDA tools, and high-end chips, reflecting new priorities and confirming industry weaknesses.

All in all, then, we observe bureaucratic adjustments to the changing realities of the industry. These reflect the capacity to learn, rather than simply replicating old policies. While Fuller (2016, 2021) is correct in pointing out continuity in these policy documents in terms of the general use of tax incentives, support for the industry, and preference for state-controlled companies, we qualify his analysis by highlighting the existence of bureaucratic adaptation and the incremental evolution of more targeted attempts to push businesses to upgrade.

While it is impossible to make definitive assessments on the effectiveness of these disciplining measures, reports indicate that many companies, often attracted by abundant (local) public funds, are still entering the industry without proper know-how (Hille & Yu, 2020; Gan, 2021). Related to this, new cases of bankruptcies and fraud have emerged, such as the Wuhan Hongxin Semiconductor Manufacturing Company, which, after acquiring enormous local funding, had to be closed down when a fraud scheme was uncovered (Gan, 2021). Another example is Beijing-based Tsinghua Unigroup, which expanded into semiconductors in the 2010s. However, without previous experience (Fuller, 2019), Unigroup ran into financial difficulties and was eventually rescued by two state-backed venture capital funds. Although some of its subsidiaries have achieved success – UNISOC is currently among the top five mobile-processor manufacturers globally – Unigroup continues to engage in activities unrelated to innovation, such as real estate (Zhang & Lan, 2023). Recently, it was revealed that top executives of the IC "Big Fund" are under investigation by the CDIC, the anti-corruption watchdog. Overall, these reports and recent developments indicate clear weaknesses in disciplining capacities, even in a top-priority industry.

These problems can be explained by examining the intersection between shortcomings in disciplining businesses and the behavior of local governments, which are still driven by the endless attraction of large-scale investments but without necessarily focusing on technological upgrading. While the EIT policies do establish a link between the amount of fiscal support and technological upgrading, other sources of state support – for example, investment funds, discounted land prices, and bank loans – are outside the purview of the policy documents examined here and are often controlled by local governments. Once again, practices from the "growth by any means" phase persist.

3.2 Electric Vehicles

The electric vehicles industry also illustrates strengths and weaknesses of the Chinese bureaucracy, although performance is better than in semiconductors. As an emerging industry, the technology for electric vehicles is characterized by greater uncertainty. Without proven market demand when the state started to promote the industry, many questions were raised about its future. However, this emerging industry was not mature anywhere and therefore did not yet have well-established incumbent leaders, thus giving the bureaucracy an opportunity to take advantage of lower barriers to entry and support a "leapfrogging" strategy. In the traditional internal combustion engine (ICE) automobile industry, in contrast, domestic firms did not manage to challenge global leaders. In the 2000s, China was still dependent on foreign technology. The national strategy of attracting FDI and forging joint ventures (JVs) with SOEs, in the hope that technology transfers and upgrading would follow, brought rather disappointing results (Lee et al., 2021). Joint ventures customarily only adapted older technologies and did not make significant investments in R & D (Thun, 2018). The hope of the Chinese leadership is that the electric vehicle industry will allow China to achieve the status of an industry leader while it is still being forged. This is a different scenario from the canonical developmental states, where countries often excelled in catching up in preexisting industries with proven market demand and lower technological uncertainty.

Electric vehicles, known in the PRC as New Energy Vehicles (NEVs), encompass different new technologies: pure battery electric, plug-in hybrid electric, and fuel cell vehicles (or hydrogen). Moreover, NEVs include different types of vehicles – private passenger cars, public and private buses, taxis, official vehicles, garbage and sanitation trucks, and logistics vehicles. The strategy for the industry initially followed four grand objectives: to promote technological upgrading in a frontier industry, to address concerns over energy security, to reduce carbon emissions, and to reduce urban pollution (Gong et al., 2013).

As the industry is emergent, technological capacities are still evolving everywhere, and so are related concerns. A significant concern of consumers worldwide is what is called "range anxiety": the worry that the battery will run out of power before a destination or charging point is reached. If this is not addressed, consumers are likely to stick to conventional ICEs (Hove & Sandalow, 2019; Taalbi & Nielsen, 2021). It is therefore critical that companies upgrade their technology to provide vehicles with a longer driving range, and that governments promote the buildup of a well-distributed network of charging stations (Hove & Sandalow, 2019; Mims, 2021). The expansion of NEVs is inextricably linked to improving these two variables. As in other countries, governmental actions also aim at reducing the penetration of ICEs and boosting NEV sales.[43]

In China, the central state has not only set targets for the quantitative expansion of the industry, but is also promoting the charging infrastructure and supporting company upgrading. As we will show, the bureaucracy has adapted to the evolution of the industry. By the early 2020s, China had clearly forged ahead of other middle-income countries, and is now increasingly a source of competitive concern for advanced economies, a scenario that is very different from both traditional automobiles and semiconductor fabrication.

3.2.1 Increased Central Bureaucratic Coherence and Industry Creation

Policies on NEVs are typically formulated by four central agencies: the NDRC, MOST, MIIT, and MOF. The initial push for NEVs came from MOST and its then minister Wan Gang, at a time when the industry was still nascent and national sales figures very low. As the industry took shape, however, the MIIT took the lead from the mid-2010s (Interviews #31, #32). This leadership is also

---

[43] On the multiple measures governments employ, see International Energy Agency (2021). In some cases, individual companies also received generous state support, such as Tesla and its 465 million US dollar loan guarantee from the US Department of Energy (Rodrik, 2014).

related to the formulation, in 2017, of the "dual-credit" policy, spearheaded by the MIIT (see Section 3.2.3). Furthermore, taking advantage of its more technocratic profile, the MIIT has assumed the task of canvassing the views of several industry experts and channeling that information into the decision-making process. The NDRC, meanwhile, has a "coordinating" role, as Zhao Wei, an expert on electric vehicle battery firms, argues (Interview #27; see also Zhao & Lüthje, 2022). Lastly, the MOF concentrates on the value of the subsidies distributed and the rules of their implementation.

A review of the main policy milestones for the industry reveals its evolution from a rather experimental and exploratory program to a more robust approach. National policies aimed at promoting NEVs started in the 1990s, when the focus was on prototype development (Gong et al., 2013; Liu & Kokko, 2013). In the 2000s, the bureaucracy started to develop more specific plans and NEVs were included in the MLP 2006, although there was still no precise policy for promoting the sector. The crucial stimulus came at the end of the 2000s. This, according to Qiang Zhi, was fueled by a policy network headed by MOST minister Wan Gang and initially based in a small office for electric vehicles at the ministry. The network of scholar-turned-official Wan Gang "continually recruited supporters to then pitch its ideas to central policymakers" (Interview #30).

In 2009, the PRC made a decisive move into commercial sales, launching the "ten cities, thousand vehicles" pilot program (Gong et al., 2013; Liu & Kokko, 2013). The initial focus was on public sector vehicles, such as public buses, taxis, and sanitation vehicles, but it soon expanded to private passenger cars. In 2012, with the "Program for Saving Energy and Developing the Automotive Industry with New Energies (2012–2020)," the State Council (2012) finally created a fixed national policy that became the basis for the promotion of NEVs until 2020, including purchase subsidies, increasingly stringent fuel economy requirements, CO_2 emission standards for ICE vehicles, guidelines for the promotion of the charging infrastructure, and tax exemptions, among others. The government's target for cumulative production and sales of NEVs was 500,000 units by 2015, and five million by the end of 2020 (State Council, 2016b). By 2025, NEVs are expected to account for around 20 percent of total annual vehicles sales (State Council, 2020b).

Although the "ten cities, thousand vehicles" and 2015 targets were missed, sales soared in the second half of the decade. With 4.92 million NEVs on the road by the end of 2020, most analysts consider the target to have been met, and China became the world's largest market. Moreover, in this period domestic companies such as BYD, NiO, and Xpeng emerged. Traditional state-owned automakers, such as SAIC and BAIC, also diversified their production toward NEVs. BYD, a vertically integrated company manufacturing a range of products, from batteries to final vehicles, is perhaps the most successful. It leads the domestic market share in the private car segment, has a reputable position in the electric buses segment – delivering units in countries such as the UK, for example – and also sells batteries to other NEV assemblers. Recently, NiO started to make inroads in Europe, although it is still too early to tell whether it will be able to compete with larger manufacturers such as Volkswagen or Stellantis. When it comes to battery production – the core component of NEVs – the PRC is now home to the largest producer in the world, CATL, which supplies MNCs such as Tesla. The average battery capacity for pure electric vehicles improved by around 23 percent between 2014 and 2019, although this still lags behind the average for the United States and Europe (Jin et al., 2021).

3.2.2 Vertical Incoherence, but Functional Experimentalism

As with other industries, local governments are very supportive of NEVs. With enough leeway to come up with their own initiatives by experimenting with local policies to boost NEV sales and promote local models, city governments, in particular, are key to understanding the growth of the industry in the 2010s. However, their actions can also sometimes be ambiguous, hampering the implementation of certain central policy objectives (He et al., 2018; Gomes et al., 2023).

Local experimentalism is illustrated by various city-level actions. For example, while some cities moved more decisively toward full electrification of their public transportation fleets, using public procurement policies (e.g., Shenzhen), others relied more on softer regulatory policies, such as free and special parking spaces and bus lane access for private passenger cars (e.g., Liuzhou; see Cui & He, 2019). Another Shenzhen innovation was to create preferential policies for electric logistics vehicles, such as vans and light trucks, which served as a template for other cities, like Suzhou (Gomes et al., 2023). Another measure, the "green plates" policy, which exempts NEVs from the otherwise mandatory auction or lottery that ICE owners must enter to obtain a new license plate, is also essentially a local issue. Given how expensive and time-consuming it can be to obtain a plate, this policy strongly incentivizes the purchase of NEVs. While some large cities took the lead on this initiative, others have never implemented it (He et al., 2018). Moreover, since the central purchase subsidy policy has a critical local component – the option for city bureaucrats to add subsidies from local coffers – cities more prone to invest in the industry usually offered the highest subsidy possible, while others were more cautious (Lauer & Liefner, 2019; Yeung, 2019).

With regard to the charging infrastructure, city bureaucracies have the autonomy to decide the value of the subsidies charging point operators are entitled to, and, assisted by local urban planning policy agencies, have the authority to plan the location of new charging points as well as the policy parameters that mandate a minimum number of parking spaces for NEVs in commercial and residential areas (Hove & Sandalow, 2019; Lauer & Liefner, 2019). Beyond this, some localities also invest in battery swap stations: instead of waiting for a full recharge, drivers can simply swap their depleted batteries for new ones, a process that is normally faster than the regular charge. This is the business model that NiO, a start-up heavily supported by the city of Hefei, has been promoting.

This local autonomy results in well-known problems, however. One of these is the duplication of investments throughout the country, generating a fragmented market and hindering the benefits of economies of scale. According to Kennedy (2020), there were 119 active NEV companies in 2020. Indeed, top MIIT officials have already expressed their dissatisfaction with this scenario, describing NEV firms as "mostly small and scattered" (Bloomberg, 2021). Relatedly, many local governments utilize protectionist measures, especially when it comes to supporting local companies for the supply of public buses and taxis (Yeung, 2019; Interview #32).

Overall, local governments have proven pivotal to promoting the industry, often supporting local companies. Lacking "blueprints" or "best practices" at the beginning of the push, Chinese cities have been actively experimenting with new policies and mechanisms to boost the NEV market. In an emerging industry where barriers to entry are still relatively low and there is scope for new models to emerge and consolidate (e.g., charging points or battery swap stations, green plates policy or fiscal subsidies), local experimentation can be beneficial. These positive attributes outweigh the drawbacks of duplication of investment and market fragmentation, at least for now. When the industry further matures, consolidation – including mergers and acquisitions and bankruptcies – will be in order.

3.2.3 Coalitions and Stronger Disciplining Mechanisms

Beyond the extension of subsidies and the other forms of state support we have described, the bureaucracy has crafted a series of partnerships between state agencies, industry, and the science system. Especially in the early stages of industry development, a series of alliances between the state, industry, and research institutes were established (Liu & Kokko, 2013; Jin et al., 2021; Zhao & Lüthje, 2022). Funded by the state, as Liu and Kokko (2013: 26) explain, these alliances "constitute important channels for communication, and can be used to influence policymakers: the lobbying taking place through the alliances may be related to standards, rules, and regulations, as well as access to infrastructure, human capital, and other resources."

To support technology transfer, specialized research centers collaborate with domestic companies. This is the case, for example, with the Tsinghua University-based "State Key Laboratory of Automotive Safety and Energy" in Beijing. In the Pearl and Yangtze River Deltas, with the aim of developing technologies in energy-saving, batteries, electric control, and autonomous driving, a number of innovation platforms were built, with the help of the New R&D Institute policy, for instance. Moreover, numerous national and local joint engineering centers, national and provincial enterprise technology centers, engineering research centers, and innovation service complexes are now home to science parks. These innovation infrastructures are superior to those of other middle-income countries, and the most cutting-edge platforms are approaching or have already reached the global frontier (Zhao & Lüthje, 2022).

The CPPCCs also play a role in the exchange of industry-specific information. In our empirical study, this particularly holds for Shenzhen, a vanguard in this respect. Members of the local CPPCC formulated policy proposals with the intention of both kick-starting and stimulating market demand for NEVs, as well as spurring technological upgrading of local firms. Preferential policies to boost market demand such as the green plates policy and reduced parking fees were discussed, as were incentives to advance the construction of a charging infrastructure in the city, including charging points and battery swap stations. Members of the CPPCC linked to local universities also urged the local government to strengthen cooperation between the industry and the science system, in particular in relation to research on autonomous driving, a technology in which Shenzhen-based Huawei is already making inroads (see the online supplementary materials).

More informal mechanisms for information exchange and consensus building are the frequent factory tours conducted by top bureaucrats. Here, bureaucrats can signal their preferences and the direction they wish companies to follow. Likewise, as one interviewee commented, it is "a great opportunity for businessmen to express disagreement in private" (Interview #32). Last, but not least, in cases of conflict higher-level party officials can and do intervene "in order to create consensus" in such circumstances (Interview #32).[44]

However, state–business–science ties also generated misallocation of capital. From 2013 to 2015, the central government spent around twenty-eight billion RMB in subsidies and local governments added another twenty billion RMB

---

[44] According to Qiang Zhi, the infamous "party schools" (often months long) are actually also platforms for training officials to develop the required expertise in industrial policymaking (Interview #30), assisted by guest industry experts, businessmen, and academics, and not just places for ideological indoctrination.

Table 3 Share of national
production of NEVs exported
(2010–2019)

Country	Share
China	1%
European Union	17%
United States	35%
Japan	66%
South Korea	74%

Source: Jin et al. (2021).

(Xu, 2021). However, not all recipient companies in the industry have long-term plans to promote technological advances, as a series of scandals in the subsidy distribution process revealed in 2016. Some companies reported inflated sales figures, entitling them to more subsidies, bribed local officials to give them fake licenses pretending they had recorded higher sales, and forged transaction receipts (ICCT, 2017).

These cases of fraud and misuse of public funds call for businesses to be disciplined. As with semiconductors, however, exports are not a suitable instrument in the NEV industry. Data for the 2010–19 period (see Table 3) reveals that accumulated exports, at a meager 1 percent, pale in comparison with other major producers. Since 2021, export performance has improved, but much of the rise is explained by Tesla's decision to export vehicles from its Shanghai factory (Sebastian & Chimits, 2022). As it stands, exports cannot be used as the key discipline mechanism.

As in semiconductors, then, the bureaucracy must employ different measures and targeted regulations to make businesses behave in accordance with the upgrading goals. Indeed, soon after the 2016 fraud schemes were exposed, the Chinese leadership announced significant changes to the subsidy program. First, more technological requirements were added, which companies had to meet to apply for subsidies. Until 2016, only the driving range (R) and the maximum speed were required for pure battery vehicles to be eligible. In 2017, minimum levels of energy efficiency and battery energy density were incorporated (ICCT, 2017; Interviews #31, #32). Increasingly, therefore, low-tech producers are being excluded from the program. These changes also reflect increased knowledge among bureaucrats of the relevant technical parameters of the industry and business reactions to state policies. Indeed, as one interviewee bluntly stated, by the early 2010s bureaucrats' "knowledge was still limited" (Interview #32); however, by 2016, when the measures discussed here were implemented, their knowledged had increased. With time, bureaucrats have learned how to adjust policies to better discipline businesses, albeit imperfectly.

Second, to reward businesses that advanced technological upgrading, the value of subsidies were more closely tied to technological parameters. Vehicles with greater technological sophistication could hence receive a higher subsidy.[45] Third, there were frequent signals that the value of subsidies was declining, indicating to firms that they needed to depend less on subsidies. Table 4 depicts these trends.

On the one hand, then, the value of subsidies decreased, especially after 2016. For example, the highest value in 2013 was 60,000 RMB, while in 2016 it was 55,000 RMB (roughly 92 percent of the 2013 value) and in 2022 it was 12,600 RMB (21 percent of the 2013 value). On the other hand, and more importantly, technical requirements became stricter. As a result, only advanced producers could enjoy the benefits of the program. Until 2016, vehicles with a driving range of 100 km were eligible for subsidies. This minimum requirement now stands at 300 km.

Additionally, new measures with the potential to reduce disciplining costs were announced. Beyond more random inspections and penalties for offenders, a requirement was introduced that nonprivate vehicles, typically buses and other (semi-)public vehicles, have to first achieve a minimum mileage of 30,000 km for companies to receive the subsidies at a later stage. Moreover, all private vehicles would be equipped with an onboard monitoring device, allowing the mileage to be recorded in real time (Cui, 2017).

Finally, and in relation to the gradual decline in importance of the subsidy program, by the end of the decade, a new program spearheaded by the MIIT – the dual-credit system – was established (ICCT, 2017; Yeung, 2019; Kennedy, 2020; Jin et al., 2021). This system sets mandatory targets for NEV production and fuel efficiency for ICEs, so that automakers without a minimum level of NEV production and below-average fuel efficiency are forced to buy credits from companies with a surplus, or face penalties. Companies that only produce NEVs, such as BYD, NiO, and Tesla, automatically benefit. In practice, this policy nudges automakers to shift their production from ICEs to NEVs, representing a subtle form of discipline. Importantly, capacities to learn from international experiences play a role here too. The dual-credit system was clearly inspired by California's Zero-Emission Vehicle Program and was the result of

---

[45] Until 2016, only the driving range (R) was used. Thereafter, battery energy density was also included. The final subsidy value is calculated using multipliers for battery energy density, energy consumption, and ownership. Formulas specifying the necessary calculations are found in the official documents used as sources for Table 4. For the sake of simplicity, we only focus on R. Our conclusions do not change when taking other technical variables into account.

Table 4 Subsidies for pure battery electric vehicles, according to driving range (R) (2013–2022)

Driving range (km)	Subsidy value (RMB)									
	2013	2014	2015	2016	2017	2018	2019	2020	2021	2022
80≤R<150	35,000	33,250	31,150	–	–	–	–	–	–	–
100≤R<150				25,000	20,000	–	–	–	–	–
150≤R<200	50,000	47,500	45,000	45,000	36,000	15,000	–	–	–	–
200≤R<250						24,000	–	–	–	–
250≤R<300	60,000	57,000	54,000	55,000	44,000	34,000	–	–	–	–
300≤R<400						45,000	18,000	16,200	13,000	9,100
R≥400						50,000	25,000	22,500	18,000	12,600

Source: Authors' elaboration, based on MOF (2013, 2016, 2019, 2020a, 2020b, 2021) and EV days (2015).

actual exchanges between Chinese and Californian experts (Jin et al., 2021). This indicates a bureaucracy that is adaptable to new realities and stands in contradiction to the image of an ossified and paralyzed system, unable to change course when necessary.[46]

Overall, these measures promote the exchange of continued state support for improvements in performance by business, the core idea behind Amsden's notion of discipline. To make these measures more effective, however, the state bureaucracy must have the human resources and capabilities to monitor and enforce their implementation. This is certainly more resource intensive and therefore more demanding for China's bureaucracy than using exports, which is an easily observed and rarely manipulated variable.

4 Conclusion

This Element has scrutinized two critical factors to examine whether recent bureaucratic reforms are capable of spurring innovation-driven development in China: first, the need to achieve internal coherence and, second, the capacity to promote coalitions and discipline domestic companies. We now summarize our key findings and, in relation to remaining research gaps and the open-ended transformations the PRC is undergoing, suggest potentially promising subjects for future research.

First, with regard to the need to forge a coherent bureaucracy at horizontal level, we find the innovation-oriented segments of the Chinese bureaucracy to have been substantially reformed. In particular, the period after the 2000s witnessed a rise in the significance of key central ministries, of which we highlight the NDRC, MIIT, and MOST. In actively promoting innovation and industrial policies, these ministries have improved their capacity to work together over time, although their power positions relative to each other vary according to the industry in question. Bureaucratic coherence has improved since the earlier reform period, and the innovation wing of the party-state works more effectively than its equivalent in other middle-income countries. However, the PRC still falls short of the ideal-type pilot agency found in the canonical developmental states. In addition, entrance to the civil service has become more competitive. These improvements have not replaced high-level patronage and other earlier, more ineffective methods of governing economic and technology affairs, but rather have been layered on top of them. For now,

---

[46] Even the fact that the 100 percent foreign-owned Tesla factory was attracted to Shanghai in 2018 is seen by industry experts as an attempt to increase the competitive pressure on domestic brands, forcing them to upgrade (Interviews #27, #31, #32). Again, the bureaucracy is adapting in order to craft better disciplining strategies.

a hybrid has developed that is nonetheless "good enough" to support many aspects of innovation.

In relation to vertical coherence, we find serious attempts to ensure local bureaucrats work in tandem with the overriding innovation goals set by the center. To address the legacies of the 1980s and 1990s – particularly implementation gaps and local noncompliance – the system that monitors local officials has been tightened and the cadre evaluation system recalibrated toward innovation targets. These reforms have seen local officials reorient toward innovation-related goals and continue with local experimentation to that end. However, two fundamental problems have not been resolved: the fiscal mismatch between revenue and expenditure at local level and the existence of multiple, at times contradictory, targets against which local bureaucrats are evaluated. By pursuing the targets of increased budgetary revenues and high-tech industrial output at the same time, for instance, local bureaucracies attracted large-scale foreign high-tech investment, thereby inhibiting the development of domestic firms. Moreover, the use of targets such as patents to evaluate performance allowed local agents to distort the relevant information. This also explains the explosion in patents since 2007, yet the concurrent low quality of many (though certainly not all). This conflict between the innovation paradigm introduced by the center and the behavior of local officials represents a central and enduring obstacle to China's innovation strategy.

Despite these obstacles, the innovation-oriented segments of the Chinese bureaucracy are far from disorganized or ossified. These segments frequently adapt to new realities, albeit imperfectly, in a learning process. Our findings thus qualify one-sided impressions that "increasingly, economic policymaking in China seems disorganized, dominated by a short-term mindset" (Minzner, 2018: 64). Admittedly, elements of short-termism and bureaucratic conflict do exist. But these are largely the hallmarks of the earlier reform era, and they are less pronounced than before. Concerted attempts to fight short-termism and lack of national coordination have left their mark – like it or not.

Second, with regard to the need to promote coalitions – to ease state–business information exchange as well as to foster science–industry collaboration – we observe the institutionalization of consultative mechanisms becoming increasingly important. We also identify a parallel trend to better integrate S & T organizations, typically in the form of innovation platforms and a variety of state–business–science partnerships. This finds expression in targeted attempts to strengthen synergies between bureaucrats primarily concerned with sector-specific industrial policies and those concerned with the buildup of broad-based innovation capabilities – as exemplified in the semiconductor and electric vehicle industries. At national level, this is reflected in the strengthened roles that both the MOST and the MIIT have assumed. Compared to the canonical developmental states, these coalitions are less centralized, less formalized, and more diverse. Moreover, the main trend remains adapting existing products and neglecting investment in more uncertain areas such as basic R & D—which are only likely to yield returns in the long run.

Disciplining mechanisms have been strengthened and adjusted. However, disciplining capabilities are not on a par with those studied by Amsden. In contrast to the South Korean case, which relied on the export performance of domestic businesses, disciplining largely involves employing bureaucratic and regulatory measures, and other more subtle forms, which sometimes appear to be less rigorous than in other contemporary developmental bureaucracies (see Maggor, 2021). While local officials are now monitored against innovation-related goals, businesses are disciplined through a set of targeted measures and regulations. Increasingly, regulations have been enacted to incentivize business to invest in R & D, and to move away from sectors such as real estate or entertainment and toward high-tech manufacturing. In fact, this seems to be part of the rationale behind Xi's recent "crackdown" on business. While industries with limited prospects of technological upgrading, such as the consumer internet industry and online short-term rental platforms, have been penalized – including giants such as Alibaba – high-tech manufacturing has largely remained unscathed. The crackdown was not an indiscriminate attack on private business as such, but clearly targeted specific sectors of the economy. In reality, as Nicholas Lardy and Tianlei Huang (2021) have argued, "the private companies hit by Beijing's regulatory tightening over the past year [2021], though among the largest in terms of size, are simply a small portion of the entire private sector in China." The crackdown is also related to the trend of forcing large businesses to realign their business models with national goals and to recent fears over "premature deindustrialization" (Huang & Yang, 2022), a malady that has hit many other economies with similar income per capita levels, especially in Latin America (Rodrik, 2016). The strong support for semiconductors and electric vehicles reflects this logic. With respect to disciplining mechanisms for these two industries, we find similar trends. Regulations and bureaucratic measures aimed at pegging technological upgrading in these industries to fiscal benefits, either in the form of subsidies or tax breaks, were implemented from the 2000s onward.

By focusing on changing state–business dynamics, and on discipline as a key category for analyzing these, we move away from mainstream categories such as "cronyism" and "predation" (e.g., Pei, 2016; Minzner, 2018). These typically assume that state and business are, or should be, two hermetically separated spheres, and that close ties between them inevitably lead to negative outcomes.

Employing the concept of discipline enables us to shed light on evolving state–business relations in contemporary China, highlighting the existence of different disciplining mechanisms, their respective advantages and shortcomings, and the presence of both positive and negative outcomes. Similarly, our research shows that, despite the clearly increasing importance of state institutions in the promotion of industrial policies and innovation, this does not necessarily imply the suppression of business or market forces. The promotion of electric vehicles is a case in point: substantial state support allowed a new industry to emerge, bringing new profit opportunities to a series of private companies that were created along the way. The state can spur the creation of whole new markets, and the relationship between the two should not be seen as always antagonistic. Additionally, it appears that despite the overall tightening of party control and surveillance under Xi Jinping, some sectors of Chinese society – those crucial to the party's self-declared goal of innovation – can operate in a reasonably business-friendly environment. Instead of waging a full-scale and indiscriminate assault on any one agent's leeway, the governing elite is selectively adjusting what is permitted and what is prohibited.

In light of the above, some conclusions on the PRC's standing in terms of innovative performance are in order. It is an inescapable fact that China has made significant progress, and is now the world's most innovative middle-income country, outpacing other large emerging economies such as Brazil, Russia, India, or South Africa. However, while selected Chinese companies are already able to operate at the global technological frontier, others are still some way behind those of advanced economies and thus unable to unilaterally dominate a wide array of high-tech sectors. Our analysis of semiconductors and electric vehicles confirms these general trends. Electric vehicle companies are currently competing at the technological frontier. Chinese semiconductor companies are, in general, nowhere near the frontier, although they have progressed significantly, certainly more than in any other middle-income country. Our sectoral comparison thus lends support to state-of-the-art econometric findings in Mao et al. (2021), namely, that China performs better in new emerging industries than in mature catch-up industries, where path dependencies such as Western control of value chains and intellectual property loom large. We also engage with Wong's (2011) study on biotech. In comparison to successful technology borrowing in earlier developmental states, Wong argues, the uncertainties in contemporary knowledge creation and innovation at the frontier hinder strategic policymaking. Bureaucrats are typically not adept at identifying the right technologies. Our findings on the electric vehicles industry qualify this argument. However, since the uncertainties and difficulties of technology creation in biotech seem to be greater than in electric vehicles, further examination of the difficulties bureaucracies encounter at various technological frontiers – in a cross-sectoral and cross-national research design – may advance our academic understanding.

Lastly, we would like to highlight some future research avenues. First, more systematic comparisons with other late developers are in order. This holds for countries with both similar and different regime types, such as Vietnam and Brazil, and for the bureaucracies of large emerging capitalist economies, in particular. Comparative assessments of contemporary upgrading capacities beyond the Organisation for Economic Co-operation and Development (OECD) are needed. Second, despite the significant data collection challenges, more fieldwork-based research is needed to answer the question of the extent to which efforts to tighten monitoring of local officials have affected the propensity of state–business coalitions to promote productive investment and of how the mechanisms of state–business–science information exchange and technology transfer have developed in the most recent period. This applies, for instance, to the role of CPPCCs and innovation intermediaries. Discipline mechanisms also deserve further study – while we focused on the allocation of subsidies and tax breaks, other areas, such as the allocation of bank loans and state-backed investment funds, should be scrutinized. The same holds for the relationship between foreign and domestic capital and the potential for productive collaboration, including attempts to disentangle how different types of FDI impact the prospects for technological upgrading differently – delicate yet necessary themes to help us better understand the potential impact of economic "decoupling" and "disengagement," particularly in areas where supply chains are long and complex. Third, in relation to our industry comparison, which followed the criteria of new emerging industries versus mature catch-up industries, it would be fruitful to engage in dialogue with other typologies, such as Hsueh's (2022) categorization of centralized versus decentralized governance in strategic and nonstrategic industries. Last, but not least, labor as well as skill formation and education systems warrant more attention. This includes the trend toward labor market polarization, a phenomenon already observed in other countries. China has a very large informal workforce, undermining stable job profiles and thus also continuous upskilling for large parts of the population.

References

Acemoglu, D. & Robinson, J. A. (2012). *Why Nations Fail: The Origins of Power, Prosperity, and Poverty*, New York: Crown Publishers.

Amsden, A. H. (1989). *Asia's Next Giant: South Korea and Late Industrialisation*, Oxford: Oxford University Press.

Andreas, J. (2009). *Rise of the Red Engineers: The Cultural Revolution and the Origins of China's New Class*, Stanford, CA: Stanford University Press.

Ang, Y. Y. (2017a). Beyond Weber: Conceptualizing an Alternative Ideal-Type of Bureaucracy in Developing Contexts. *Regulation & Governance*, **11**(3), 282–98.

Ang, Y. Y. (2017b). Do Weberian Bureaucracies Lead to Markets or Vice-Versa? A Coevolutionary Approach to Development. In A. Kohli, D. Yashar, & M. Centeno, eds., *States in the Developing World*, Cambridge: Cambridge University Press, 280–306.

Ang, Y. Y. (2020). *China's Gilded Age: The Paradox of Economic Boom and Vast Corruption*, New York: Cambridge University Press.

Appelbaum, R., Cao, C., Han, X., Parker, R., & Simon, D. (2018). *Innovation in China: Challenging the Global Science and Technology System*, Cambridge: Polity Press.

Appelbaum, R., Gebbie, M., Han, X., Stocking, G., & Kay. L (2016). Will China's Quest for Indigenous Innovation Succeed? Some Lessons from Nanotechnology. *Technology in Society*, **46**, 149–63.

Armanios, D. E. & Eesley, C. E. (2021). How Do Institutional Carriers Alleviate Normative and Cognitive Barriers to Regulatory Change? *Organization Science*, **32**(6), 1415–38. https://pubsonline.informs.org/doi/10.1287/orsc.2021.1434.

Bachman, D. M. (1985). *Chen Yun and the Chinese Political System*, Berkeley: Institute of East Asian Studies, University of California.

Baek, S. (2005). Does China Follow "the East Asian Development Model"? *Journal of Contemporary Asia*, **35**(4), 485–98.

Baum, R. & Shevchenko, A. (1999). The State of the State. In M. Goldman & R. MacFarquhar, eds., *The Paradox of China's Post-Mao Reforms*, London: Harvard University Press, 333–62.

Beeson, M. (2009). Developmental States in East Asia: A Comparison of the Japanese and Chinese Experiences. *Asian Perspective*, **33**(2), 5–39.

Blecher, M. & Shue, V. (2001). Into Leather: State-Led Development and the Private Sector in Xinji. *China Quarterly*, **166**, 368–93.

Bloomberg (2021). China Vows to Consolidate the Bloated Electric Vehicle Industry. *Bloomberg News*, September 13. https://bit.ly/3nT4wW6. Last accessed: August 13, 2022.

Boeing, P., Eberle, J., & Howell, A. (2022). The Impact of China's R&D Subsidies on R&D Investment, Technological Upgrading and Economic Growth. *Technological Forecasting and Social Change*, **174**, 121212. https://doi.org/10.1016/j.techfore.2021.121212.

Breznitz, D. & Murphree, M. (2011). *The Run of the Red Queen: Government, Innovation, Globalization, and Economic Growth in China*, New Haven, CT: Yale University Press.

Burns, J. (1994). Strengthening Central CCP Control of Leadership Selection: The 1990 Nomenklatura. *China Quarterly*, **138**, 458–91.

Burns, J. (1999). The People's Republic of China at 50: National Political Reform. *China Quarterly*, **159**, 580–94.

Burns, J. & Wang, X. (2010). Civil Service Reform in China: Impacts on Civil Servants' Behaviour. *China Quarterly*, **201**, 58–78.

Butollo, F. & ten Brink, T. (2018). Domestic Market Growth and Local State Support in the Upgrading of China's LED Lighting Industry. *Global Networks*, **18**(2), 285–306.

Cao, C. & Suttmeier, R. P. (2017). Challenges of S&T System Reform in China. *Science*, **355**(6329), 1019–21.

Cartier, C. (2001). "Zone Fever", the Arable Land Debate, and Real Estate Speculation: China's Evolving Land Use Regime and Its Geographical Contradictions. *Journal of Contemporary China*, **10**(28), 445–69.

Centeno, M., Kohli, A., Yashar, D. J. & Mistree, D. (eds.) (2017). *States in the Developing World*, Cambridge: Cambridge University Press.

Chan, H. & Li, S. (2007). Civil Service Law in the People's Republic of China: A Return to Cadre Personnel Management. *Public Administration Review*, **67**(3), 383–98.

Chang, H. J. (2002). Breaking the Mould: An Institutionalist Political Economy Alternative to the Neo-Liberal Theory of the Market and the State. *Cambridge Journal of Economics*, **26**(5), 539–59.

Chang, H. J. (2006). *The East Asian Development Experience: The Miracle, the Crisis and the Future*, New York: Zed Books.

Chen, H. & Rithmire, M. (2020). The Rise of the Investor State: State Capital in the Chinese Economy. *Studies in Comparative International Development*, **55**(3), 257–77.

Chen, J., Yin, X., Fu, X., & McKern, B. (2021). Beyond Catch-Up: Could China Become the Global Innovation Powerhouse? China's Innovation Progress and Challenges from a Holistic Innovation Perspective. *Industrial and Corporate Change*, **30**(4), 1037–64.

Chen, L. (2017). Grounded Globalization: Foreign Capital and Local Bureaucrats in China's Economic Transformation. *World Development*, **98**, 381–99.

Chen, L. (2018). *Manipulating Globalization: The Influence of Bureaucrats on Business in China*, Stanford, CA: Stanford University Press.

Chen, L. & Yang, W. (2019). R&D Tax Credits and Firm Innovation: Evidence from China. *Technological Forecasting and Social Change*, **146**(September), 233–41.

Chen, M. (2015). From Economic Elites to Political Elites: Private Entrepreneurs in the People's Political Consultative Conference. *Journal of Contemporary China*, **24**(94), 613–27.

Chen, M. & Huang, D. (2019). The Institutional Origin of Private Entrepreneurs' Policy Influence in China: An Analysis of the All-China Federation of Industry and Commerce. *Journal of Chinese Governance*, **4**(3), 267–91.

Chen, T. J. (2016). The Development of China's Solar Photovoltaic Industry: Why Industrial Policy Failed. *Cambridge Journal of Economics*, **40**, 755–74.

Chen, T. J. & Ku, Y. H. (2014). Indigenous Innovation vs. Teng-long Huan-niao: Policy Conflicts in the Development of China's Flat Panel Industry. *Industrial and Corporate Change*, **23**(6), 1445–67.

Chibber, V. (1999). Building a Developmental State: The Korean Case Reconsidered. *Politics & Society*, **27**(3), 309–46.

Chibber, V. (2003). *Locked in Place: State-Building and Late Industrialization in India*, Princeton, NJ: Princeton University Press.

Chin, G. (2018). The Evolution of Government–MNC Relations in China: The Case of the Automotive Sector. In X. Zhang & T. Zhu, eds., *Business, Government and Economic Institutions in China*, Basingstoke: Palgrave Macmillan, 81–104.

Cho, H. (2005). *Chinas langer Marsch in den Kapitalismus*, Münster: Westfälisches Dampfboot.

Christmann-Budian, S. (2012). Chinesische Wissenschaftspolitik seit den 1990er Jahren: Eine empirische Untersuchung zur praxispolitischen und ideologischen Funktionalisierung von Wissenschaft in einer transformativen Gesellschaft der Globalisierungsära. PhD thesis, Freie Universität Berlin.

Chung, J. H. (2000). *Central Control and Local Discretion in China: Leadership and Implementation during Post-Mao Decollectivization*, Oxford: Oxford University Press.

Chung, J. H. (2015). China's Local Governance in Perspective: Instruments of Central Government Control, *China Journal*, **75**, 38–60.

Cohen, W., Nelson, R., & Walsh, J. (2000). Protecting Their Intellectual Assets: Appropriability Conditions and Why U.S. Manufacturing Firms Patent (or Not). NBER Working Paper No. 7552, February 19.

Conlé, M., Kroll, H., Storz, C., & ten Brink, T. (2023). University Satellite Institutes as Exogenous Facilitators of Technology Transfer Ecosystem Development. *Journal of Technology Transfer*, **48**(1), 147–80.

Conlé, M., Zhao, W., & ten Brink, T. (2021). Technology Transfer Models for Knowledge-Based Regional Development: New R&D Institutes in Guangdong, China. *Science and Public Policy*, **48**(1), 132–44.

Cortese, A. (2022). China's Tech Pivot (Part I): From Behemoth Platforms to Little Giants. MacroPolo, March 22. https://macropolo.org/chinas-tech-pivot-behemoth-platforms-little-giants/. Last accessed: July 20, 2022.

Cui, H. (2017). Subsidy Fraud Leads to Reforms for China's EV Market. International Council on Clean Transportation, May 30. https://theicct.org/sub sidy-fraud-leads-to-reforms-for-chinas-ev-market/. Last accessed: July 21, 2022.

Cui, H. & He, H. (2019). Liuzhou: A New Model for the Transition to Electric Vehicles? International Council on Clean Transportation, December 18. https://theicct.org/liuzhou-a-new-model-for-the-transition-to-electric-vehicles/. Last accessed: July 21, 2022.

de Graaff, N., ten Brink, T., & Parmar, I. (2020). China's Rise in a Liberal World Order in Transition. *Review of International Political Economy*, **27**(2), 191–207.

Deng, G. & Kennedy, S. (2010). Big Business and Industry Association Lobbying in China: The Paradox of Contrasting Styles. *China Journal*, **63** (January), 101–25.

Dickson, B. (2008). *Wealth into Power: The Communist Party's Embrace of China's Private Sector*, New York: Cambridge University Press.

Dominguez Lacasa, I., Jindra, B., Radosevic, S., & Shubbak, M. (2019). Paths of Technology Upgrading in the BRICS Economies. *Research Policy*, **48** (1), 262–80.

Donaldson, J. A. (2017). China's Administrative Hierarchy: The Balance of Power and Winners and Losers within China's Levels of Government. In J. A. Donaldson, ed., *Assessing the Balance of Power in Central–Local Relations in China*, Abingdon, UK: Routledge, 105–37.

Doner, R. F. (1992). Limits of State Strength: Toward an Institutionalist View of Economic Development. *World Politics*, **44**(3), 398–431.

Doner, R. F. & Schneider, B. R. (2000). Business Associations and Economic Development: Why Some Associations Contribute More Than Others. *Business and Politics*, **2**(3), 261–88.

Doner, R. F. & Schneider, B. R. (2016). The Middle-Income Trap: More Politics Than Economics. *World Politics*, **68**(4), 1–37.

Doner, R. F., Ritchie, B. K., & Slater, D. (2005). Systemic Vulnerability and the Origins of Developmental States: Northeast and Southeast Asia in Comparative Perspective. *International Organization*, **59**(2), 327–61.

Drummond, C. (2022). A produção local de semicondutores volta a ser debatida. *Carta Capital*, December 31. www.cartacapital.com.br/economia/a-producao-local-de-semicondutores-volta-a-ser-debatida/. Last accessed: February 8, 2023.

Duchâtel, M. (2021). The Weak Links in China's Drive for Semiconductors. Institut Montaigne Policy Paper.

Duckett, J. (2001). Bureaucrats in Business, Chinese-Style: The Lessons of Market Reform and State Entrepreneurialism in the People's Republic of China. *World Development*, **29**(1), 23–37.

Edin, M. (2003). State Capacity and Local Agent Control in China: CCP Cadre Management from a Township Perspective. *China Quarterly*, **173**, 35–52.

Edler, J. & Fagerberg, J. (2017). Innovation Policy: What, Why, and How. *Oxford Review of Economic Policy*, **33**(1), 2–23.

EV days (2015). *2016-2020 Xin nengyuan qiche butie zhengce quan jiedu* [2016–2020 New Energy Vehicle Subsidy Policy Full Interpretation], April 30. www.evdays.com/html/2015/0430/zc49387.html. Last accessed: August 14, 2022.

Evans, P. (1995). *Embedded Autonomy: States and Industrial Transformation*, Princeton, NJ: Princeton University Press.

Ezell, S. (2021). *Moore's Law under Attack: The Impact of China's Policies on Global Semiconductor Innovation*, Information Technology & Innovation Foundation. https://itif.org/publications/2021/02/18/moores-law-under-attack-impact-chinas-policies-global-semiconductor/.

Fan, C. L. & Li, Z. (2022) Orientation and Role of National Scientific Research Institutions in National Strategic Scientific and Technological Strength. *Bulletin of Chinese Academy of Sciences*, **37**(5), 642–51 (in Chinese).

Fischer, D., Gohli, H., & Habich-Sobiegalla, S. (2021). Industrial Policies under Xi Jinping: A Steering Theory Perspective. *Issues & Studies* **57**(4), 2150016. http://doi.org/10.1142/S1013251121500168.

Fu, X. (2015). *China's Path to Innovation*, Cambridge: Cambridge University Press.

Fu, X., McKern, B., & Chen, J. (2022). *The Oxford Handbook of China Innovation*, New York: Oxford University Press.

Fuller, D. (2016). *Paper Tiger, Hidden Dragons: Firms and the Political Economy of China's Technological Development*, Oxford: Oxford University Press.

Fuller, D. (2019). Growth, Upgrading and Limited Catch-Up in China's Semiconductor Industry. In L. Brandt & T. Rawski, eds., *Policy, Regulation and Innovation in China's Electricity and Telecom Industries*, Cambridge: Cambridge University Press, 262–303.

Fuller, D. (2021). China's Counter-Strategy to American Export Controls in Integrated Circuits. *China Leadership Monitor*, **67**. http://dx.doi.org/10.2139/ssrn.3798291.

Gallagher, K. P. & Shafaeddin, M. (2010). Policies for Industrial Learning in China and Mexico. *Technology in Society*, **32**(2), 81–99.

Gan, H. T. (2021). Semiconductor Fraud in China Highlights Lack of Accountability. *Nikkei Times*, February 12. http://bit.ly/3Wc2RaV. Last accessed: November 12, 2021.

Gang, F. & Woo, W. T. (2009). The Parallel Partial Progression (PPP) Approach to Institutional Transformation in Transition Economies: Optimize Economic Coherence, Not Policy Sequence. *Modern China*, **35**(4), 352–69.

Gao, Y., Hu, Y., Liu, X., & Zhang, H. (2021). Can Public R&D Subsidy Facilitate Firms' Exploratory Innovation? The Heterogeneous Effects between Central and Local Subsidy Programs. *Research Policy*, **50**(4), 104221.

Gereffi, G. (2009). Development Models and Industrial Upgrading in China and Mexico. *European Sociological Review*, **25**(1), 37–51.

Global Innovation Index. (2022). *Global Innovation Index 2022: What Is the Future of Innovation Driven Growth?* www.globalinnovationindex.org/home.

Göbel, C. & Heberer, T. (2017). The Policy Innovation Imperative: Changing Techniques for Governing China's Local Governors. In V. Shue & P. Thornton, eds., *To Govern China: Evolving Practices of Power*, Cambridge: Cambridge University Press, 279–304.

Gomes, A. P., Pauls, R., & ten Brink, T. (2023). Industrial Policy and the Creation of the Electric Vehicles Market in China: Demand Structure, Sectoral Complementarities and Policy Coordination. *Cambridge Journal of Economics*, **47**(1), 45–66. https://doi.org/10.1093/cje/beac056.

Gong, H., Wang, M. Q., & Wang, H. (2013). New Energy Vehicles in China: Policies, Demonstration, and Progress. *Mitigation and Adaptation Strategies for Global Change*, **18**(2), 207–28.

Grimes, S. & Du, D. (2022). China's Emerging Role in the Global Semiconductor Value Chain. *Telecommunications Policy*, **46**(2), 101959. https://doi.org/10.1016/j.telpol.2020.101959.

Grünberg, N. & Drinhausen, K. (2019). *The Party Leads on Everything: China's Changing Governance in Xi Jinping's New Era*. MERICS China Monitor, September 24. https://merics.org/sites/default/files/2020-05/The%20Party%20leads%20on%20everything_0.pdf.

Guangdong Department of Industry and Information Technology (GDIIT) (2016). *Dongguan jicheng dianlu chanye fazhan baipishu* [Dongguan IC Industry Development White Paper].

Haggard, S. (2018). *Developmental States*, Cambridge: Cambridge University Press.

Hamadeh, N., van Rompaey, C., Metreau, E., & Eapen, S. G. (2022) New World Bank Country Classifications by Income Level: 2022–2023. https://blogs.worldbank.org/opendata/new-world-bank-country-classifications-income-level-2022-2023.

Han X. & Appelbaum R. P. (2018). China's Science, Technology, Engineering, and Mathematics (STEM) Research Environment: A Snapshot. *PloS ONE*, **13**(4), e0195347. https://doi.org/10.1371/journal.pone.0195347.

He, H., Jin, L., Cui, H., & Zhou, H. (2018). Assessment of Electric Car Promotion Policies in Chinese Cities. International Council on Clean Transportation, October 18. https://theicct.org/publication/assessment-of-electric-car-promotion-policies-in-chinese-cities/. Last accessed: July 21, 2022.

Heberer, T. & Schubert, G. (2019). Weapons of the Rich: Strategic Behavior and Collective Action of Private Entrepreneurs in China. *Modern China*, **45**(5), 471–503.

Heffer, A. & Schubert, G. (2023). Policy Experimentation under Pressure in Contemporary China. *China Quarterly*, **253**, 35–56. http://doi.org/10.1017/S0305741022001801.

Heilmann, S. (2008). Policy Experimentation in China's Economic Rise. *Studies on Comparative International Development*, **43**, 1–26.

Heilmann, S. (2017). *China's Political System*, Lanham, MD: Rowman & Littlefield.

Heilmann, S. & Shih, L. (2013). The Rise of Industrial Policy in China, 1978–2012. Harvard-Yenching Institute Working Paper.

Heilmann, S., Shih, L., & Hofem, A. (2013). National Planning and Local Technology Zones: Experimental Governance in China's Torch Programme. *China Quarterly*, **216**, 896–919.

Hille, K. & Yu, S. (2020). Chinese Groups Go from Fish to Chips in New Author's "Great Leap Forward." *Financial Times*, October 13. www.ft.com/content/46edd2b2-1734-47da-8e77-21854ca5b212. Last accessed: June 12, 2021.

Hove, A. & Sandalow, D. (2019). *Electric Vehicle Charging in China and the United States*, Columbia School of International and Public Affairs, Center of Global Energy Policy.

Howell, J. (2006). Reflections on the Chinese state. *Development and Change*, **37**(2), 73–97.

Hsueh, R. (2022). *Micro-Institutional Foundations of Capitalism: Sectoral Pathways to Globalization in China, India, and Russia*, Cambridge: Cambridge University Press.

Hu, A., Zhang, P., & Zhao, L. (2017). China as Number One? Evidence from China's Most Recent Patenting Surge. *Journal of Development Economics*, **124**, 107–19.

Huang, H. (ed.) (2021). *China's Industrial Policy Transformation: Theory and Practice*. Singapore: World Scientific.

Huang, Q. & Yang, H. (2022). Zhongguo zhizao ye bizhong "neiwai cha" xianxiang ji qi "qu gongyehua" hanyi. [The phenomenon of "internal and external difference" in the proportion of China's manufacturing industry and its meaning for "de-industrialization"]. *Zhongguo gongye jingji* [*China Industrial Economy*], March. www.hybsl.cn/zonghe/zuixinshiliao/2022-03-31/74749.html.

Huang, T. & Lardy, N. (2021). Is the Sky Really Falling for Private Firms in China? Peterson Institute for International Economics, October 14. www.piie.com/blogs/china-economic-watch/sky-really-falling-private-firms-china. Last accessed: July 21, 2022.

Huang Y. (1996). Central–Local Relations in China during the Reform Era: The Economic and Institutional Dimensions. *World Development*, **24**(4), 655–72.

Huang, Y. (2002). Between Two Coordination Failures: Automotive Industrial Policy in China with a Comparison to Korea. *Review of International Political Economy*, **9**(3), 538–73.

Hui, M. (2022). China Has Big Economic Plans for Its "Little Giant" Companies. *Quartz*, March 16. https://qz.com/2142761/china-has-big-economic-plans-for-little-giant-companies/. Last accessed: July 20, 2022.

Hung, H. F. (2015). *The China Boom: Why China Will Not Rule the World*, New York: Columbia University Press.

ICCT. (2017). *Adjustment to Subsidies for New Energy Vehicles in China*. International Council on Clean Transportation, May. https://theicct.org/sites/default/files/publications/China-NEV_ICCT_policy-update_17052017_vF.pdf. Last accessed: July 21, 2022.

International Energy Agency (2021). *Global EV Outlook 2021*.

Jiang, R., Shi, H., & Jefferson, G. (2020). Measuring China's International Technology Catchup. *Journal of Contemporary China*, **29**(124), 519–34.

Jin, L., He, H., Cui, H., et al. (2021). *Driving a Green Future: A Retrospective Review of China's Electric Vehicle Development and Outlook for the Future*, International Council on Clean Transportation, Washington, DC. https://theicct.org/sites/default/files/publications/China-green-future-ev-jan2021.pdf. Last accessed: May 19, 2023.

Johnson, C. (1982). *MITI and the Japanese Miracle: The growth of Industrial Policy, 1925–1975*, Stanford, CA: Stanford University Press.

Johnson, C. (1999). The Developmental State: Odyssey of a Concept. In M. Woo-Cumings, ed., *The Developmental State*, London: Cornell University Press, 32–60.

Johnson, C., Kennedy, S., & Qiu, M. (2017). Xi's Signature Governance Innovation: The Rise of Leading Small Groups. Center for Strategic and International Studies, October 17. www.csis.org/analysis/xis-signature-govern ance-innovation-rise-leading-small-groups. Last accessed: July 20, 2022.

Kang, D. C. (2002). *Crony Capitalism: Corruption and Development in South Korea and the Philippines*, New York: Cambridge University Press.

Kay, C. (2002). Why East Asia Overtook Latin America: Agrarian Reform, Industrialisation and Development. *Third World Quarterly*, **23**(6), 1073–1102.

Kennedy, S. (2005). *The Business of Lobbying in China*, Cambridge: Harvard University Press.

Kennedy, S. (2020). The Coming NEV War? Implications of China's Advances in Electric Vehicles. Center for Strategic and International Studies, November 18. www.csis.org/analysis/coming-nev-war-implications-chinas-advances-electric-vehicles. Last accessed: July 21, 2022.

Khan, M. H. (2010). Political Settlements and the Governance of Growth-Enhancing Institutions. Unpublished manuscript. https://eprints.soas.ac.uk/9968/1/Political_Settlements_internet.pdf.

Khan, M. H. (2012). Beyond Good Governance: An Agenda for Developmental Governance. In K. S. Jomo & A. Chowdhury, eds., *Is Good Governance Good for Development?*, London: Bloomsbury Academic, 151–82.

Kim, S. Y. (2020). East Asia's Developmental States in Evolution: The Challenge of Sustaining National Competitiveness at the Technological Frontier. In E. Vivares, eds., *The Routledge Handbook to Global Political Economy: Conversations and Inquiries*, London: Routledge, 511–27.

Kleinhans, J. P. & Baisakova, N. (2020). *The Global Semiconductor Value Chain: A Technology Primer for Policy Makers*, Stiftung Neue Verantwortung, Berlin. www.stiftung-nv.de/de/publikation/global-semiconductor-value-chain-technol ogy-primer-policy-makers. Last accessed: May 19, 2023.

Klingler-Vidra, R. & Wade, R. (2020). Science and Technology Policies and the Middle-Income Trap: Lessons from Vietnam. *Journal of Development Studies*, **56**(4), 717–31.

Knight, J. B. (2014). China as a Developmental State. *The World Economy*, **37**(10), 1335–47.

Kohli, A. (2004). *State-Directed Development: Political Power and Industrialisation in the Global Periphery*, New York: Cambridge University Press.

Kostka, G. & Yu, X. (2015). Career Backgrounds of Municipal Party Secretaries in China: Why So Few Municipal Party Secretaries Rise from the County Level? *Modern China*, **41**(5), 467–505.

Kroeber, A. (2016). *China's Economy: What Everyone Needs to Know*, London: Oxford University Press.

Krueger, A. O. (1990). Government Failures in Development. *Journal of Economic Perspectives*, **4**(3), 9–23.

Lauer, J. & Liefner, I. (2019). State-Led Innovation at the City Level: Policy Measures to Promote New Energy Vehicles in Shenzhen, China. *Geographical Review*, **109**(3), 436–56.

Lee, J. & Kleinhans, J. P. (2021). *Mapping China's Semiconductor Ecosystem in Global Context: Strategic Dimensions and Conclusions.* MERICS and Stiftung Neue Verantwortung, June 30, 2021. https://merics.org/en/report/ mapping-chinas-semiconductor-ecosystem-global-context-strategic-dimen sions-and-conclusions. Last accessed: May 19, 2023.

Lee, K. (2022). How Realistic Are China's Semiconductor Ambitions? *Project Syndicate*, June 27. www.project-syndicate.org/commentary/china-semicon ductor-industry-leapfrog-us-competition-by-keun-lee-2022-06. Last accessed: July 21, 2022.

Lee, K., Qu, D., & Mao, Z. (2021). Global Value Chains, Industrial Policy, and Industrial Upgrading: Automotive Sectors in Malaysia, Thailand, and China in Comparison with Korea. *European Journal of Development Research*, **33**(2), 275–303.

Lee, S. (2017). An Institutional Analysis of Xi Jinping's Centralization of Power. *Journal of Contemporary China*, **26**(105), 325–36.

Leftwich, A. (2010). Beyond Institutions: Rethinking the Role of Leaders, Elites and Coalitions in the Institutional Formation of Developmental States and Strategies. *Forum for Development Studies*, **37**(1), 93–111.

Leslie, S. (2000). The Biggest "Angel" of Them All: The Military and the Making of Silicon Valley. In M. Kenney, ed., *Understanding Silicon Valley: The Anatomy of an Entrepreneurial Region*, Stanford, CA: Stanford University Press, 48–67.

Leutert, W. & Eaton, S. (2021). Deepening Not Departure: Xi Jinping's Governance of China's State-owned Economy. *China Quarterly*, **248**, 1–22.

Li, C. & Yang, Z. (2015). What Causes the Local Fiscal Crisis in China: The Role of Intermediaries. *Journal of Contemporary China*, **24**(94), 573–93.

Li, H. & Zhou, L. A. (2005). Political Turnover and Economic Performance: The Incentive Role of Personnel Control in China. *Journal of Public Economics*, **89**(9–10), 1743–62.

Lieberthal, K. & Lampton, D. M. (1992). *Bureaucracy, Politics, and Decision Making in Post-Mao China*, Berkeley: University of California Press.

Lin, K.-C. (2007). With Strings Attached? Improving the Administration of Central State Financed Investment Projects in the PRC. *Asian Journal of Political Science*, **15**(3), 319–43.

Liu, M. & Tsai, K. (2021). Structural Power, Hegemony, and State Capitalism: Limits to China's Global Economic Power. *Politics & Society*, **49**(2), 235–67.

Liu, X., Schwaag Serger, S., Tagscherer, U., & Chang, A. Y. (2017). Beyond Catch-Up – Can a New Innovation Policy Help China Overcome the Middle Income Trap? *Science and Public Policy*, **44**(5), 656–69.

Liu, Y. & Kokko, A. (2013). Who Does What in China's New Energy Vehicle Industry? *Energy Policy*, **57**, 21–29.

Liu, Z. (2008). Foreign Direct Investment and Technology Spillovers: Theory and Evidence. *Journal of Development Economics*, **85**, 176–93.

Lu, X. (2000). Booty Socialism, Bureau-Preneurs, and the State in Transition: Organizational Corruption in China. *Comparative Politics*, **32**(3), 273–94.

Maggor, E. (2021). The Politics of Innovation Policy: Building Israel's "Neo-developmental" State. *Politics & Society*, **49**(4), 451–87.

Mao, J., Tang, S., Xiao, Z., & Zhi, Q. (2021). Industrial Policy Intensity, Technological Change, and Productivity Growth: Evidence from China. *Research Policy*, **50**(7), 104287. https://doi.org/10.1016/j.respol.2021.104287.

May, C., Nölke, A., & ten Brink, T. (2019). Public–Private Coordination in Large Emerging Economies: The Case of Brazil, India and China. *Contemporary Politics*, **25**(3), 276–91.

Mazzucato, M. (2016). From Market Fixing to Market-Creating: A New Framework for Innovation Policy. *Industry and Innovation*, **23**(2), 140–56.

Mei, C. & Pearson, M. M. (2014). Killing a Chicken to Scare the Monkeys? Deterrence Failure and Local Defiance in China. *China Journal*, **72**, 75–97.

Mertha, A. (2005). China's "Soft" Centralization: Shifting Tiao/Kuai Authority Relations. *China Quarterly*, **184**, 791–810.

Migdal, J. (1988). *Strong Societies and Weak States: State Society Relations and State Capabilities in the Third World*, Princeton, NJ: Princeton University Press.

Miller, A. L. (2014). More Already on the Central Committee's Leading Small Groups. *China Leadership Monitor*, 44. www.hoover.org/sites/default/files/research/docs/clm44am.pdf. Last accessed: August 4, 2022.

Miller, A. L. (2020). Xi Jinping and the Evolution of Chinese Leadership Politics. In T. Fingar & J. C. Oi, eds., *Fateful Decisions: Choices That Will Shape China's Future*, Stanford, CA: Stanford University Press, 33–50.

Mims, C. (2021). What's Missing in the Electric-Vehicle Revolution: Enough Places to Plug In. *Wall Street Journal*, February 27. https://bit.ly/3pSQJj5. Last accessed: May 19, 2023.

Minzner, C. (2018). *End of an Era: How China's Authoritarian Revival Is Undermining Its Rise.* New York: Oxford University Press.

MOF (2013). *Guanyu jixu kaizhan xin nengyuan qiche tuiguang yingyong gongzuo de tongzhi* [Notice on Continuing the Promotion and Application of New Energy Vehicles], September 13.

MOF (2015). *Guanyu wanshan yanjiu kaifa feiyong shui qian jia ji kouchu zhengce de tongzhi* [Notice on Improving the Pre-tax Deduction Policy for Research and Development Expenses], November 2. www.chinatax.gov.cn/n810341/n810755/c1878881/content.html. Last accessed: August 14, 2022.

MOF (2016). *Guanyu tiaozheng xin nengyuan qi chetui guang ying yong caizheng butie zhengce de tongzhi* [Notice on Adjusting the Financial Subsidy Policy for the Promotion and Application of New Energy Vehicles], December 29.

MOF (2019). *Guanyu jinyibu wanshan xin nengyuan qiche tuiguang yingyong caizheng butie zhengce de tongzhi* [Notice on Further Improving the Financial Subsidy Policy for the Promotion and Application of New Energy Vehicles], March 26.

MOF (2020a). *Guanyu wanshan xin nengyuan qiche tuiguang yingyong caizheng butie zhengce de tongzhi* [Notice on Improving the Financial Subsidy Policy for the Promotion and Application of New Energy Vehicles], April 23.

MOF (2020b). *Guanyu jinyibu wanshan xin nengyuan qiche tuiguang yingyong caizheng butie zhengce de tongzhi* [Notice on Further Improving the Financial Subsidy Policy for the Promotion and Application of New Energy Vehicles], December 31.

MOF (2021). *Guanyu 2022 nian xin nengyuan qiche tuiguang yingyong caizheng butie zhengce de tongzhi* [Notice on the Promotion and Application of Financial Subsidy Policies for New Energy Vehicles in 2022], December 31.

Montero, A. P. (2001). Delegative Dilemmas and Horizontal Logics: Subnational Industrial Policy in Spain and Brazil. *Studies in Comparative International Development*, **36**(3), 58–89.

Moore, M. & Schmitz, H. (2008). Idealism, Realism and the Investment Climate in Developing Countries. IDS Working Paper 307.

Moore, S. (2014). Hydropolitics and Inter-Jurisdictional Relationships in China: The Pursuit of Localized Preferences in a Centralized System. *China Quarterly*, **219**, 760–80.

Müller, A. (2017). Cooperation of Vocational Colleges and Enterprises in China. Working Papers on East Asian Studies, Duisburg-Essen University.

Mungiu-Pippidi, A. (2020). The Rise and Fall of Good-Governance Promotion. *Journal of Democracy*, **31**(1), 88–102.

Nahm, J. (2017). Exploiting the Implementation Gap: Policy Divergence and Industrial Upgrading in China's Wind and Solar Sectors. *China Quarterly*, **231**, 705–27.

Naughton, B. (1995). *Growing Out of the Plan: Chinese Economic Reform 1978–1993*, Cambridge: Cambridge University Press.

Naughton, B. (2018). *The Chinese Economy: Adaptation and growth*, Cambridge, MA: MIT Press.

Naughton, B. (2020). Grand Steerage. In T. Fingar & J. C. Oi, eds., *Fateful Decisions. Choices That Will Shape China's Future*, Stanford, CA: Stanford University Press, 51–81.

Naughton, B. (2021). *The Rise of China's Industrial Policy, 1978 to 2020*. National Autonomous University of Mexico. https://dusselpeters.com/ CECHIMEX/Naughton2021_Industrial_Policy_in_China_CECHIMEX .pdf.

NBS (2020a). *Zhongguo tongji nianjian* [China Statistical Yearbook], Beijing: Zhongguo tongji chubanshe [China Statistics Press].

NBS (2020b). *Zhongguo keji tongji nianjian* [China Statistical Yearbook on Science and Technology], Beijing: Zhongguo tongji chubanshe [China Statistics Press].

NBS (various years). *Zhongguo tongji nianjian* [China Statistical Yearbook], Beijing: Zhongguo tongji chubanshe [China Statistics Press].

Nölke, A., ten Brink, T., Claar, S., & May, C. (2020). *State-Permeated Capitalism in Large Emerging Economies*, Basingstoke: Routledge.

O'Brien, K. J. & Li, L. (1999). Selective Policy Implementation in Rural China. *Comparative Politics*, **31**(2), 167–86.

OECD. (2005). *Oslo Manual: Guidelines for Collecting and Interpreting Innovation Data*, 3rd ed., The Measurement of Scientific and Technological Activities, OECD Publishing, Paris. https://bit.ly/3OLvM3Z.

Oi, J. (1995). The Role of the Local State in China's Transitional Economy. *China Quarterly*, **144**, 1132–49.

Oi, J. (2020). Future of Central–Local Relations. In T. Fingar & J. C. Oi, eds., *Fateful Decisions. Choices That Will Shape China's Future*, Stanford, CA: Stanford University Press, 107–27.

Oliveira, F. (2020). Governo encaminha extinção da CEITEC em seu melhor momento [Government Conducts the Closure of CEITEC at Its Best Moment]. *A Revolução Industrial Brasileira*, November 23. https://rib.ind

.br/governo-encaminha-extincao-da-ceitec-em-seu-melhor-momento/. Last accessed: February 8, 2023.

Ong, L. (2012). Between Developmental and Clientelist States: Local State–Business Relationships in China. *Comparative Politics*, **44**(2), 191–209.

Pack, H. & Saggi, K. (2006). Is There a Case for Industrial Policy? A Critical Survey. *World Bank Research Observer*, **21**(2), 267–97.

Painter, M. (2012) "Poor Governance" for Development in China and Vietnam. In K. S. Jomo and A. Chowdhury, eds., *Is Good Governance Good for Development?*, London: Bloomsbury, 135–50.

Pan, F., Zhang, F., & Wu, F. (2021). State-Led Financialization in China: The Case of the Government-Guided Investment Fund. *China Quarterly*, **247**, 749–72.

Paus, E. (2020). Innovation Strategies Matter: Latin America's Middle-Income Trap Meets China and Globalisation. *Journal of Development Studies*, **56**(4), 657–79.

Pei, M. (2016). *China's Crony Capitalism: The Dynamics of Regime Decay*, Cambridge, MA: Harvard University Press.

Pirie, I. (2013). Globalization and the Decline of the Developmental State. In B. Fine, J. Saraswati, & D. Tavasci, eds., *Beyond the Developmental State: Industrial Policy into the Twenty-first Century*, London: Pluto Press, 146–68.

Polanyi, K. (2001). *The Great Transformation: The Political and Economic Origins of Our Time*, Boston, MA: Beacon Press.

Postiglione, G. A. (2020). Expanding Higher Education: China's Precarious Balance. *China Quarterly*, **244**, 920–41.

Qu, T. (2021). US–China Tech War: AI, Semiconductors Get Quasi-Military Commanders as "Supply Chain Chiefs" to Boost Self-Sufficiency. *South China Morning Post*, June 26. www.scmp.com/tech/tech-war/article/3138785/us-china-tech-war-ai-semiconductors-get-quasi-military-commanders. Last accessed: November 12, 2021.

Rithmire, M. & Chen, H. (2021). The Emergence of Mafia-Like Business Systems in China. *China Quarterly*, **248**(1), 1037–58.

Rodrik, D. (2014). Green Industrial Policy. *Oxford Review of Economic Policy*, **30**(3), 469–91.

Rodrik, D. (2016). Premature Deindustrialization. *Journal of Economic Growth*, **21**, 1–33.

Sagild, R. & Ahlers, A. (2019). Working for Harmony and Innovation? Political Inclusion of Diversified Elites via the Chinese People's Political Consultative Conference. Forum Internationale Wissenschaft, Working Paper No. 10/2019.

Saich, A. (2015). *Governance and Politics of China*, London: Palgrave Macmillan.

SBIIT. (2021). 2020 nian Suzhou Shi jicheng dianlu chanye fazhan baipishu [2020 Suzhou IC Industry Development White Paper]. Suzhou Bureau of Industry and Information Technology.

Schmid, J. & Wang, F. (2017). Beyond National Innovation Systems: Incentives and China's Innovation Performance. *Journal of Contemporary China*, **26**(104), 280–96.

Schneider, B. R. & Maxfield, S. (1997). Business, the State, and Economic Performance in Developing Countries. In S. Maxfield & B. R. Schneider, eds., *Business and the State in Developing Countries*, Ithaca, NY: Cornell University Press, 3–35.

Schneider, R. (1998). Review: Elusive Synergy: Business–Government Relations and Development. *Comparative Politics*, **31**(1), 101–22.

Sebastian, G. & Chimits, F. (2022) "Made in China" Electric Vehicles Could Turn Sino–EU Trade on Its Head. MERICS, May 30. https://merics.org/en/comment/made-china-electric-vehicles-could-turn-sino-eu-trade-its-head.

Shambaugh, D. L. (2008). *China's Communist Party: Atrophy and Adaptation*, Berkeley: University of California Press.

Shen, C., Jin, J., & Zou, H. F. (2012). Fiscal Decentralization in China: History, Impact, Challenges and Next Steps. *Annals of Economics and Finance*, **13**(1), 1–51.

Shen, Y., Yu J., & Zhou, J. (2020). The Administration's Retreat and the Party's Advance in the New Era of Xi Jinping: the Politics of the Ruling Party, the Government, and Associations in China. *Journal of Chinese Political Science*, **25**, 71–88.

Shih, V., Adolph, C., & Liu, M. (2012). Getting Ahead in the Communist Party: Explaining the Advancement of Central Committee Members in China. *American Political Science Review*, **106**(1), 166–87.

Shirk, S. (1993). *The Political Logic of Economic Reform in China*, Berkeley: University of California Press.

Shue, V. (1994). State Power and Social Organization in China. In J. Migdal, A. Kohli, & V. Shue, eds., *State Power and Social Forces: Domination and Transformation in the Third World*, New York: Cambridge University Press, 65–88.

Sinha, A. (2003). Rethinking the Developmental State Model: Divided Leviathan and Subnational Comparisons in India. *Comparative Politics*, **35**(4), 459–76.

Slodkowski, A. (2022). Chip Supplier Says China Will Struggle to Develop Advanced Technology. *Financial Times*, May 22. www.ft.com/content/a3e2c685-2f1f-46cf-892b-c44cdda88919. Last accessed: July 20, 2022.

SMIC (various years). *SMIC Annual Report*. https://www.smics.com/en/site/ company_financialSummary

Smith, G. (2015). Getting Ahead in Rural China: The Elite Cadre Divide and Its Implications for Rural Governance. *Journal of Contemporary China*, **24**(94), 594–612.

State Council (2000). *Guowuyuan guanyu yinfa guli ruanjian chanye he jicheng dianlu chanye fazhan ruogan zhengce de tongzhi* [Circular of the State Council on Issuing Several Policies for Encouraging the Development of the Software Industry and Integrated Circuit Industry], June 24.

State Council (2011). *Guowuyuan guanyu yinfa jinyibu guli ruanjian chanye he jicheng dianlu chanye fazhan ruogan zhengce de tongzhi* [Circular of the State Council on Issuing Several Policies for Further Encouraging the Development of the Software Industry and the Integrated Circuit Industry], February 9.

State Council (2012). *Guowuyuan guanyu yinfa jieneng yu xin nengyuan qiche chanye fazhan guihua* [State Council's Notice on Energy-Saving and New Energy Vehicles Industry Development Plan (2012–2020)], July 9. www.gov .cn/zwgk/2012-07/09/content_2179032.htm. Last accessed: August 14, 2022.

State Council (2016a). *Guojia chuangxin qudong fazhan zhanlüe gangyao* [Outline of the National Innovation-Driven Development Strategy], May 19. www.xinhuanet.com/politics/2016-05/19/c_1118898033.htm. Last accessed: August 14, 2022

State Council (2016b). *Guowuyuan guanyu yinfa 'shisanwu' guojia zhanlüe xing xinxing chanye fazhan guihua de tongzhi* [Notice of the State Council on Issuing the National Strategic Emerging Industry Development Plan for the 13th Five-Year Plan], November 29, www.gov.cn/zhengce/content/2016-12/ 19/content_5150090.htm. Last accessed: August 14, 2022.

State Council (2019). *Guanyu zai zhiding xingzheng fagui guizhang xingzheng guifanxing wenjian guocheng zhong chongfen xiqu qiye he hangye xiehui shanghui yijian de tongzhi* [Notification about Comprehensively Seeking the Opinion of Sectoral and Entrepreneurial Associations When Specifying Administrative and Regulatory Documents and Decrees], March 1. www .gov.cn/zhengce/content/2019-03/13/content_5373423.htm. Last accessed: November 12, 2021.

State Council (2020a). *Guowuyuan guanyu yinfa xin shiqi cujin jicheng dianlu chanye he ruanjian chanye gao zhiliang fazhan ruogan zhengce de tongzhi* [Circular of the State Council on Issuing Several Policies for Promoting the High-quality Development of the Integrated Circuit Industry and the Software Industry in the New Era], July 27.

State Council (2020b). *Guowuyuan bangong ting guanyu yinfa xin nen-gyuan qiche chanye fazhan guihua (2021–2035) de tongzhi* [Notice of the General Office of the State Council on Printing and Distributing the New Energy Vehicle Industry Development Plan (2021–2035)], October 20.

State Intellectual Property Office (2022). *Guojia zhishi chanquan ju:2025 Nian yiqian quanbu quxiao dui zhuanli shouquan de ge lei caizheng xing zizhu* [State Intellectual Property Office: Before 2025, All Kinds of Financial Subsidies for Patent Authorization Will Be Cancelled], January 27. www.gov.cn/xinwen/2022-01/27/content_5670755.htm. Last accessed: July 20, 2022.

Stiglitz, J. (1996). Some Lessons from the East Asian Miracle. *World Bank Researcher Observer*, **11**(2), 151–77.

Storz, C., ten Brink, T., & Zou, N. (2021). Innovation in Emerging Economies: How Do University–Industry Linkages and Public Procurement Matter for Small Businesses? *Asia Pacific Journal of Management*, **39**, 1439–80.

Su, F. & Tao, R. (2017). The China Model Withering? Institutional Roots of China's Local Developmentalism. *Urban Studies*, **54**(1), 230–50.

Sun, P. (2007). Is the State-Led Industrial Restructuring Effective in Transition China? Evidence from The Steel Sector. *Cambridge Journal of Economics*, **31**, 601–24.

Sun, X., Zhu, J., & Wu, Y. (2014). Organizational Clientelism: An Analysis of Private Entrepreneurs in Chinese Local Legislatures. *Journal of East Asian Studies*, **14**(1), 1–29.

Sun, Y. & Cao, C. (2021). Planning for Science: China's "Grand Experiment" and Global Implications. *Humanities and Social Sciences Communications*, **8**(1), 1–9.

Sutherland, D. & Ning, L. (2015). The Emergence and Evolution of Chinese Business Groups: Are Pyramidal Groups Forming? In B. Naughton & K. Tsai, eds., *State Capitalism, Institutional Adaptation, and the Chinese Miracle*, New York: Cambridge University Press, 102–53.

Sutter, K. (2021). *China's New Semiconductor Policies: Issues for Congress*, Congressional Research Service, R46767, April 20.

Suttmeier, R. P. (2020). Chinese Science Policy at a Crossroads. *Issues in Science and Technology*, **36**(2), 58–63.

SZICC [National IC Design Shenzhen Industrial Centre] (2012). Shenzhen–Hong Kong Cooperation. www.szicc.net/xmgl/sghz/. Last accessed: November 12, 2021.

Taalbi, J. & Nielsen, H. (2021). The Role of Energy Infrastructure in Shaping Early Adoption of Electric and Gasoline Cars. *Nature Energy*, **6**(10), 970–76.

Teets, J. C. (2013). Let Many Civil Societies Bloom: The Rise of Consultative Authoritarianism in China. *China Quarterly*, **213**, 19–38.

Teets, J. C. (2015). The Politics of Policy Innovation in China: Local Officials as Policy Entrepreneurs. *Issues and Studies*, **51**(2), 79–109.

ten Brink, T. (2019). *China's Capitalism: A Paradoxical Route to Economic Prosperity*, Philadelphia: University of Pennsylvania Press.

The Economist (2020). How ASML Became Chipmaking's Biggest Monopoly, February 29. www.economist.com/business/2020/02/29/how-asml-became-chipmakings-biggest-monopoly. Last accessed: July 21, 2022.

The Economist (2021). IMEC Offers Neutral Ground amid Chip Rivalries, September 23. http://bit.ly/45hTF8Q. Last accessed: May 19, 2023.

Thun, E. (2018). Innovation at the Middle of the Pyramid: State Policy, Market Segmentation, and the Chinese Automotive Sector. *Technovation*, **70–71**, 7–19.

Tsai, K. (2006). Adaptive Informal Institutions and Endogenous Institutional Change in China. *World Politics*, **59**(1), 116–41.

Tsai, K. & Cook, S. (2005). Developmental Dilemmas in China: Socialist Transition and Late Liberalization. In S. Pekkanen & K. Tsai, eds., *Japan and China in the World Political Economy*, London: Routledge, 45–66.

Tsang, S. (2009). Consultative Leninism: China's New Political Framework. *Journal of Contemporary China*, **18**(62), 865–80.

TSMC (2020). TSMC Annual Report 2020. https://investor.tsmc.com/sites/ir/annual-report/2020/2020Annual%20Report_E_%20.pdf.

TSMC (various years). TSMC Annual Reports. https://investor.tsmc.com/english/annual-reports.

Tsui, K. Y. (2011). China's Infrastructure Investment Boom and Local Debt Crisis. *Eurasian Geography and Economics*, **52**(5), 686–711.

UMC (2020). UMC Financial Review. www.umc.com/en/Download/financial_statements.

van Aken, T. & Lewis, O. A. (2015). The Political Economy of Noncompliance in China: The Case of Industrial Energy Policy. *Journal of Contemporary China*, **24**(95), 798–822.

Wade, R. (1990). *Governing the Market: Economic Theory and the Role of Government in East Asian Industrialization*, Princeton, NJ: Princeton University Press.

Wade, R. (2005). Bringing the State Back In: Lessons from East Asia's Development Experience. IPG 2 (International Politics and Society). www.fes.de/ipg/IPG2_2005/ROBERTWADE.PDF.

Walter, A. & Zhang, X. (2012). *East Asian Capitalism: Diversity, Continuity, and Change*, Oxford: Oxford University Press.

Wang. H. (2022). "Security Is a Prerequisite for Development": Consensus-Building toward a New Top Priority in the Chinese Communist Party. *Journal of Contemporary China*. https://doi.org/10.1080/10670564.2022.2108681.

Wang, J. & Mou, Y. (2021). The Paradigm Shift in the Disciplining of Village Cadres in China: From Mao to Xi. *China Quarterly*, **248**(S1), 181–99.

Wang, Y. (2019). Policy Articulation and Paradigm Transformation: The Bureaucratic Origin of China's Industrial Policy. *Review of International Political Economy*, **28**(1),204–31.

Weber, I. M. (2021). *How China Escaped Shock Therapy: The Market Reform Debate*, London: Routledge.

Wedeman, A. (2020). Anticorruption Forever? In. T. Fingar & J. C. Oi, eds., *Fateful Decisions: Choices That Will Shape China's Future*, Stanford, CA: Stanford University Press, 82–106.

Wei, Y. D. (2015). Zone Fever, Project Fever: Economic Transition, Development Policy, and Urban Expansion in China. *Geographical Review*, **105**, 156–77.

White, G. (1993). *Riding the Tiger: The Politics of Economic Reform in Post-Mao China*. Stanford, CA: Stanford University Press.

Whiting, S. (2001). *Power and Wealth in Rural China: The Political Economy of Institutional Change*, Cambridge: Cambridge University Press.

Whiting, S. (2004). The Cadre Evaluation System at the Grassroots. In B. J. Naughton & D. L. Yang, eds., *Holding China Together: Diversity and National Integration in the Post-Deng Era*, New York: Cambridge University Press, 101–19.

Wong, C. (2009). Rebuilding Government for the 21st Century: Can China Incrementally Reform the Public Sector? *China Quarterly*, **200**, 929–52.

Wong, C. H. (2021). Xi Jinping's Eager-to-Please Bureaucrats Snarl His China Plans. *Wall Street Journal*, March 7. www.wsj.com/articles/xi-jinpings-eager-to-please-minions-snarl-his-china-plans-11615141195. Last accessed: November 12, 2021.

Wong, J. (2011). *Betting on Biotech: Innovation and the Limits of Asia's Developmental State*. Ithaca, NY: Cornell University Press.

Woo-Cumings, M. (1999). Introduction: Chalmers Johnson and the Politics of Nationalism and Development. In M. Woo-Cumings, ed., *The Developmental State*. Ithaca, NY: Cornell University Press, 1–31.

World Bank. (1994). *Governance: The World Bank's Experience*. Washington, DC: World Bank.

Xu, J. (2021). Characteristics of Industry Policy on New Energy Vehicles and the Practice Research. In H. Huang, ed., *China's Industrial Policy Transformation: Theory and Practice*, Singapore: World Scientific, 257–76.

Yang, C. H. & Lee, W.-C. (2021). Establishing Science Parks Everywhere? Misallocation in R&D and Its Determinants of Science Parks in China. *China Economic Review*, **67**, 101605. http://doi.org/10.1016/j.chieco.2021.101605.

Yang, D. L. (2004). *Remaking the Chinese Leviathan: Market Transition and the Politics of Governance in China*, Stanford, CA: Stanford University Press.

Yang, X. & Yan, J. (2018). Top-Level Design, Reform Pressures, and Local Adaptations: An Interpretation of the Trajectory of Reform since the 18th CPC Party Congress. *Journal of Chinese Governance*, **3**(1), 25–48.

Yeung, G. (2019). "Made in China 2025": The Development of a New Energy Vehicle Industry in China. *Area Development and Policy*, **4**(1), 39–59.

Yu, J., Guan, K. X., Li, Z., & Chen, F. (2020). Focus on Key Technology Breakthroughs, and Strengthen National Scientific and Technological Innovation Systematization Capability. *Bulletin of Chinese Academy of Sciences*, **35**(8), 1018–23 [in Chinese].

Zeng, D. Z. (2011). How Do Special Economic Zones and Industrial Clusters Drive China's Rapid Development? Policy Research Working Paper No. WPS 5583, World Bank, Washington, DC. https://documents1.worldbank .org/curated/en/310891468018256346/pdf/WPS5583.pdf.

Zhang, C. (2019). Asymmetric Mutual Dependence between the State and Capitalists in China. *Politics & Society*, **47**(2), 149–76.

Zhang, L. & Lan, T. (2023). The New Whole State System: Reinventing the Chinese State to Promote Innovation. *Environment and Planning A: Economy and Space*, **55**(1), 201–21.

Zhang, X. (2017). Implementation of Pollution Control Targets: Has a Centralized Enforcement Approach Worked? *China Quarterly*, **231**, 749–74.

Zhang, X. (2018). Business–State-Interactions and Technology Development Regimes: A Comparative Analysis of Two Metropolises. In X. Zhang & T. Zhu, eds., *Business, Government and Economic Institutions in China*, Basingstoke: Palgrave Macmillan, 313–40.

Zhang, X. (2023). State Policy Regimes and Associational Roles in Technology Development: A Tale of Two Metropolises. *Politics & Society*, **51**(1), 30–65.

Zhang, Y., Chen, K., & Fu, X. (2019). Scientific Effects of Triple Helix Interactions among Research Institutes, Industries and Universities. *Technovation*, **86–87**, 33–47.

Zhao, W. & Lüthje, B. (2022). Value Chain Advantage from Below: A Study on How Chinese Electric Vehicle Battery Firms Build Core Competency. Unpublished manuscript.

Zhi, Q. & Pearson, M. M. (2017). China's Hybrid Adaptive Bureaucracy: The Case of the 863 Program for Science and Technology. *Governance*, **30**(3), 407–24.

Zhou, X. (2010). The Institutional Logic of Collusion among Local Governments in China. *Modern China*, **36**(1), 47–78.

Zhou, X. (2020). Organizational Response to COVID-19 Crisis: Reflections on the Chinese Bureaucracy and Its Resilience. *Management and Organization Review*, **16**(3), 473–84.

Zhou, Y. & Liu, X. (2016). Evolution of Chinese State Policies on Innovation. In Y. Zhou, W. Lazonick, & Y. Sun, eds., *China as An Innovation Nation*, Oxford: Oxford University Press, 33–67.

Acknowledgments

The authors wish to thank the anonymous reviewers of this book, as well as Meg Rithmire, Victor Shih, Ben Ross Schneider, and Rachel Beatty Riedl, who provided excellent feedback in an author workshop. We also benefited enormously from the criticisms, suggestions, and support of Armin Müller, Peter in der Heiden, Michael Schedelik, Wang Fei, Carla Welch, and Marcus Conlé. Lastly, we would like to thank Jingchun Lin for her excellent research assistance. The work was funded by a research grant from the Deutsche Forschungsgemeinschaft DFG (German Research Foundation, grant number: TE 1069/6-1).

Cambridge Elements

Politics of Development

Rachel Beatty Riedl
Einaudi Center for International Studies and Cornell University

Rachel Beatty Riedl is the Director and John S. Knight Professor of the Einaudi Center for International Studies and Professor in the Government Department and School of Public Policy at Cornell University. Riedl is the author of the award-winning *Authoritarian Origins of Democratic Party Systems in Africa* (2014) and co-author of *From Pews to Politics: Religious Sermons and Political Participation in Africa* (with Gwyneth McClendon, 2019). She studies democracy and institutions, governance, authoritarian regime legacies, and religion and politics in Africa. She serves on the Editorial Committee of *World Politics* and the Editorial Board of *African Affairs, Comparative Political Studies, Journal of Democracy,* and *Africa Spectrum*. She is co-host of the podcast Ufahamu Africa.

Ben Ross Schneider
Massachusetts Institute of Technology

Ben Ross Schneider is Ford International Professor of Political Science at MIT and Director of the MIT-Brazil program. Prior to moving to MIT in 2008, he taught at Princeton University and Northwestern University. His books include *Business Politics and the State in 20th Century Latin America* (2004), *Hierarchical Capitalism in Latin America* (2013), *Designing Industrial Policy in Latin America: Business-Government Relations and the New Developmentalism* (2015), and *New Order and Progress: Democracy and Development in Brazil* (2016). He has also written on topics such as economic reform, democratization, education, labor markets, inequality, and business groups.

Advisory Board
Yuen Yuen Ang, *University of Michigan*
Catherine Boone, *London School of Economics*
Melani Cammett, *Harvard University* (former editor)
Stephan Haggard, *University of California, San Diego*
Prerna Singh, *Brown University*
Dan Slater, *University of Michigan*

About the Series
The Element series Politics of Development provides important contributions on both established and new topics on the politics and political economy of developing countries. A particular priority is to give increased visibility to a dynamic and growing body of social science research that examines the political and social determinants of economic development, as well as the effects of different development models on political and social outcomes.

Cambridge Elements ≡

Politics of Development

Elements in the Series

Coercive Distribution
Michael Albertus, Sofia Fenner and Dan Slater

Participation in Social Policy: Public Health in Comparative Perspective
Tulia G. Falleti and Santiago L. Cunial

Undocumented Nationals
Wendy Hunter

Democracy and Population Health
James W. McGuire

Rethinking the Resource Curse
Benjamin Smith and David Waldner

Greed and Guns: Imperial Origins of the Developing World
Atul Kohli

Everyday Choices: The Role of Competing Authorities and Social Institutions in Politics and Development
Ellen M. Lust

Locked Out of Development: Insiders and Outsiders in Arab Capitalism
Steffen Hertog

Power and Conviction:The Political Economy of Missionary Work in Colonial-Era Africa
Frank-Borge Wietzke

Varieties of Nationalism: Communities, Narratives, Identities
Harris Mylonas and Maya Tudor

Criminal Politics and Botched Development in Contemporary Latin America
Andreas E. Feldmann and Juan Pablo Luna

A Chinese Bureaucracy for Innovation-Driven Development?
Alexandre De Podestá Gomes and Tobias ten Brink

A full series listing is available at: www.cambridge.org/EPOD

Printed in the United States
by Baker & Taylor Publisher Services